The Penny Whistle™ TRAVELING With Kids Book

Whether by Boat, Train, Car, or Plane—
How to Take the Best Trip Ever
with Kids of All Ages

ILLUSTRATED &
DESIGNED BY
JILL WEBER

BY

Meredith Brokaw
and Annie Gilbar

PICNIC AREA

PENNY

D1279435

A FIRESIDE BOOK PUBLISHED BY SIMON & SCHUSTER   NEW YORK, LONDON, TORONTO, SYDNEY, TOKYO, SINGAPORE

FIRESIDE
Rockefeller Center
1230 Avenue of the Americas
New York, New York 10020

FIRESIDE and colophon are registered trademarks
of Simon & Schuster Inc.

Designed by JILL WEBER
Manufactured in the United States of America

10 9 8 7 6 5 4 3 2 1

Library of Congress Cataloging-in-Publication Data

Brokaw, Meredith.
   The Penny Whistle traveling with kids book : whether by boat, train, car, or plane –
how to take the very best trip ever with kids of all ages / by Meredith Brokaw and Annie Gilbar;
illustrated and designed by Jill Weber.
      p. cm.
"A Fireside book."
   1. Travel. 2. Children – Travel. 3. Family recreation. I. Gilbar, Annie. II. Weber, Jill. III. Title.
G151.B757 1995
910'. 2'02–dc20   94-3604
                                                                                          CIP

ISBN: 0-671-88135-3
      0-671-88136-1 (pbk.)

TO ALL OUR KIDS

Jennifer, Andrea, Sarah,
Lisa, Remy, and Marc –
all of whom have
traveled near and far
and usually well

Other Penny Whistle Books:

The Penny Whistle Party Planner
The Penny Whistle Lunch Box Book
The Penny Whistle Halloween Book
The Penny Whistle Christmas Party Book
The Penny Whistle Birthday Party Book
The Penny Whistle Sick-in-Bed Book

Acknowledgments

The Brokaws
The Gilbars
The Webers
The Anthony Family
Esther Ancoli Barbasch
Joel and Irene Bennett
Peter and Maggie Bicknell, Genevieve, Jess, and
     Owen
Paul, Terry, and Lee Bilsky
Sharon, Adam, and Julia Boorstin
Paddy Calistro, Genevieve, and David McAuley
Erin, Colin, and Ruth Corey
Susan Dolgen
Cliff Einstein
Penny and Blake Epstein
Mathea Falco
Steve, Murray, and Lillian Feldman
Lorrie Goddard and Chelsea
Ronna and Joshua Gordon
Joanne Greenberg, Aaron, Ben, and Coby
Elizabeth, Jodi, and Lynda Guber
Dorian Hastings
Hildy Gottlieb Hill, Joanna, and Miranda
Andrea Hirshhorn
Hyatt Hotels

Sonia, David, and Sarah Israel
Adam and Miki Jaeger
Jan, Adam, Cara, and Jake Levine
Nancy Lynch
Jenny MacKenzie
Kim Marshall, Grand Wailea Resort, Maui, Hawaii
Elaine Mercer and Joprin Chiffy
Ellen, Jennifer, and Sarah Meyer
Sydny, Bobby, and Johnny Miner
Mary and Frank Swertlow, Nicholas and Megen
Teresa Nathanson
Nancy Perry
Cokie, Lee, and Rebecca Roberts
Al and Wanda McDaniel Ruddy, John and Ali
Jan Sargeant
Marshall Schulman
Julie Shapiro and Danny and Travelcorps
Diane, Bryn, and Neil Simon
Mary Slawson, Laurette, and Paul
Maggie Moss Tucker, Jonathan and Jennie
Dr. Peter Waldstein
Armin Weitzman
Sally and Laura Yow
and especially Beth Yow

Contents

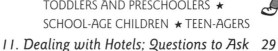
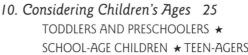

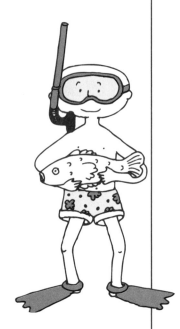

Introduction

⭐ When the Ancoli kids were little, their dad gave them a map one day and told them they could be the navigators for a day trip. Dad got into the car and drove wherever the kids told him to go. They even got to spend the night in a strange town, and then returned home the next day. It was one of the most memorable trips they ever had!

Dizzying. That's the only way to describe our busy lives. For a while, it seems as though our children will never get out of diapers, through preschool, past the school-age car pools and soccer games to become young adults, but they do. And then, when they reminisce about their childhoods, family trips and vacations stand out.

Vacations are times for family togetherness without the pressures of everyday life. Life slows down momentarily when the daily routine is suspended. Relationships are nourished and more time can be spent paying attention to individual needs. Everyone is receptive to encountering new places, people, and activities, and doing it all together. Where you go on vacation is not as important as just going somewhere together as a family. Even day trips qualify as vacations. Jennifer, Andrea, and Sarah were 7, 5, and 3 when the Brokaws took them from Los Angeles by train on a one-day excursion to the San Diego Zoo. The two older children, twenty years later, can still recall the details of that day, which included a mad scramble to catch the train on the return leg of the journey. (Sarah doesn't think she was there.)

If you can appreciate the future importance of the vacation in your child's memory bank, it is likely that the planning and execution of these trips will take on new importance. To this day, Lisa and Marc Gilbar recount in great detail their first trip to France when they were 9 and 4 and were allowed to stay up late and eat in open-air cafés with the grownups (and wasn't it amazing that Mom and Dad could actually speak French with the other diners?). They completely forgot the long trip over the Atlantic, remembering only the special treats and spending lots of time with their parents. This book is meant to help add to your own ideas about making travel with children fun for all members of the family, so that the outstanding memories down the road are all pleasant ones.

The Penny Whistle Traveling with Kids Book, the latest in our series, has everything you need to plan and execute a memorable and delightful vacation with your children. How can you ensure that a trip will be a success for everyone? It's so simple. Think of traveling with your child as your opportunity to experience new things at the same time as your children.

And if you start when the kids are quite young (say 2 years old or more) by taking short trips not far from home, by the time they're a big 5 or 6, they'll be seasoned travelers ready to hit the road. But no matter what age your children are, they'll need to be kept happily occupied and feel as though they are a part of the vacation, not just along for the ride. Nobody wants to put up with anxious, restless, bored children. (Jill Weber once counted Remy asking "Are we there yet?" nearly forty times during a two-hour trip to visit his Grandma Barbara on Cape Cod.) In fact, our own experiences traveling with our children are still fresh in our minds and hearts — both the fond memories and hard lessons learned. As in all our Penny Whistle books, we also talked to many parents who have traveled happily with their children all over the world. You'll find many stories and ideas on what works (and tips on what to avoid) in *The Penny Whistle Traveling with Kids Book.*

We include a section called Rules of the Road — thoughts and suggestions about making your vacation with your children the best it can be. You will also find The Travel Box, The Tot Backpack (for 2-, 3-, and 4-year-olds), The End-of-the-Day Box, The Travel Backpack, The Travel First-Aid Kit, and over forty games that can be played in a car, in the airplane, at a hotel, or at Grandma's house.

Traveling by car, which is the way most of us vacation, means that there will be frequent stops along the way. To make these easier and more productive, we have included a chapter on exercises you and the kids can do while on the road and a list of Road Foods and Roadside Picnics (including recipes). At the end of the book, there is a large Resource section, where you will find a list of children's museums and other attractions that children are bound to want to experience; a list of useful telephone numbers for finding destinations like dude ranches and major amusement parks; a list of books and travel guides having to do with traveling with children; a children's travel guide, activity, and game booklist; tapes for the road; and story books about flying for the first time and flying alone.

So off you go. Wheels up. Seat belts fastened. Up, up, and away. Ready, set, go. Anchors a-weigh. ***Have fun — and don't forget to write!***

✳ As our own children begin to leave the nest and start their lives without us, it occurs to us that the lessons and skills they learned when we traveled as families on how to deal with new places and people are coming in handy in their new lives.

14

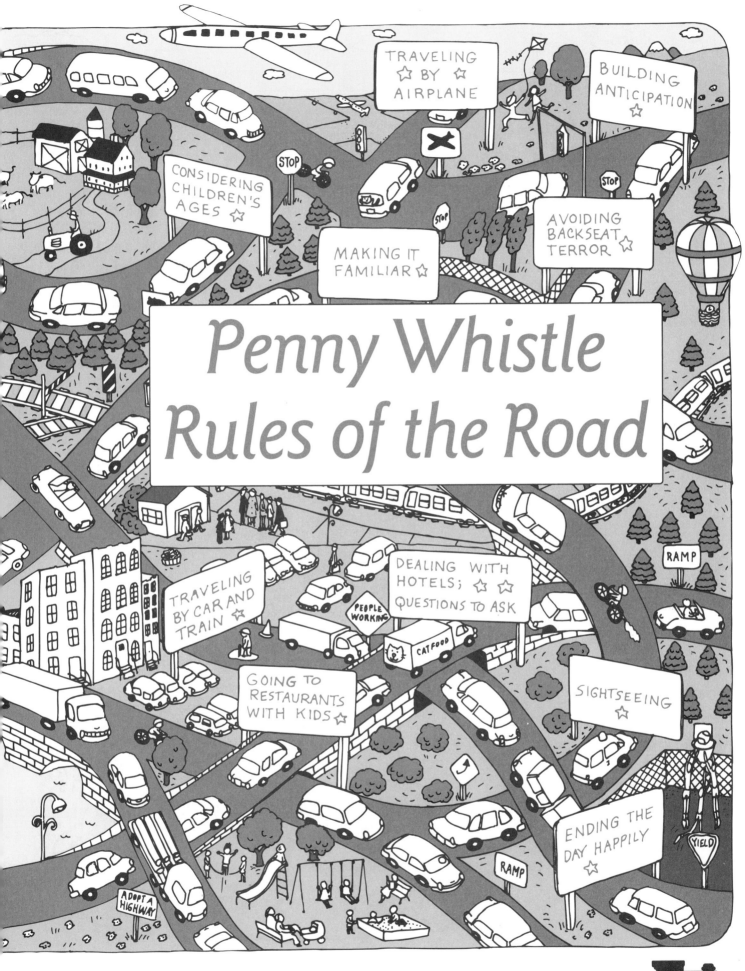

TRAVELING ☆ BY ☆ AIRPLANE

BUILDING ANTICIPATION ☆

CONSIDERING CHILDREN'S AGES ☆

AVOIDING BACKSEAT TERROR ☆

MAKING IT FAMILIAR ☆

STOP

Penny Whistle Rules of the Road

TRAVELING BY CAR AND TRAIN ☆

DEALING WITH HOTELS; ☆ ☆ QUESTIONS TO ASK

PEOPLE WORKING

CAT FOOD

RAMP

SIGHTSEEING ☆

GOING TO RESTAURANTS WITH KIDS ☆

ENDING THE DAY HAPPILY ☆

RAMP

YIELD

ADOPT A HIGHWAY

15

★ *During your trip, your child will absorb what he wants when he wants.*

★ *Says Julie Shapiro, "We learned early on to plan our trip around the boys' schedule rather than the other way around. Adults can always have a great time doing kids' activities, much more so than kids trying to participate in adults' interests."*

I. Making It Your Child's Vacation

What makes family vacations work? Careful planning, of course, but beyond that, a recognition that they are different from solo vacations or couple vacations. Family vacations work best when they are planned around the interests and developmental levels of the children who are going on them. Planning the kind of trip parents took before they were parents just won't work; but if you design a trip around your children's interests, personalities, and ages, you will be on your way to guaranteeing an unforgettable shared experience.

When you are planning to take a vacation with your children, think of it as your children's vacation. *Before any plans are made, recognize that the success of this trip revolves around your child(ren) having a good time.* Advises veteran parent Cokie Roberts, "We wanted to see another museum. Rebecca wanted a circus. We went to the circus, and had the happiest time of the entire trip."

Jan Levine and her kids — Adam, Cara, and Jake — take trips together often. Watching three kids is not easy, so Jan has come up with her own solution. The children all wear the same bright-colored hats, and always set a meeting place in case someone gets lost — not just at Disneyland but even at the local movie theater.

2. Planning with Your Child

Plan ahead but don't over-orchestrate. Leave room for spontaneity and some time for unstructured play each day.

A vacation itinerary that rolls with the punches, giving your children (as well as yourselves) time and opportunity to make on-the-spot choices and change plans, and lets you react to unforeseen encounters will allow for surprises along the way. Remembers Julie Shapiro (who is a mother and whose travel agency, Travelcorps, specializes in family travel), "The first time we took Danny on a trip to Mexico he was 7. Our schedule only allowed half hour for lunch. But Danny made friends with a child at another table, and a half hour turned into an hour, and then some. But when lunch was over, we had a happy, excited child ready to go on another adventure. Who cared if we missed the marketplace?"

Peter and Maggie Bicknell and their three children take a family vacation every year. During the year they have a "travel jar" in the kitchen; everyone is encouraged to put in loose change or money earned from chores whenever they can. This way, the children feel that they contribute to financing the vacation.

★ *When visiting a museum, negotiate 15 minutes of Renoir for 15 minutes of knights in armor.*

3. Keeping Goals Modest

Keep your goals more modest than they would be if the kids weren't with you. You may cover fewer miles and see fewer scenic attractions (and certainly fewer museums!), but the potential for whining will be considerably lower as well! Seasoned traveler Sharon Boorstin has a rule: "We only see one museum a day, and that for only one hour, when it first opens. That has always resulted in the kids' really paying attention to what they were seeing, knowing that it was a finite time at the museum, and soon we would be on the beach or playing tennis."

4. Planning Carefully

Planning well ensures success. Give research assignments to all the family members (even a very young child can draw a picture of where he will be going and what he thinks he wants to do when he gets there). They can order brochures, maps, and other literature that will inform you about your destination. The more facts and pictures everybody absorbs beforehand, the more the excitement and anticipation will build for the trip, and the adventure will be even more meaningful when you arrive. Lisa Gilbar's consistent refrain on a trip to Paris as she passed one monument after another was, "Just like in the book, Mom." And her familiarity with the little French dictionary (with more pictures than words) that she carried with her gave her an added feeling of great authority and pride when she could understand *"Bonjour, mademoiselle!"*

When a child chooses a destination or a side trip, ask him to find out for himself as much as possible about that place ahead of time. This gives a child an investment in the excursion. Try holding some informal family meetings a few weeks before the trip to talk about what's ahead and to make plans; this can also provide important lessons in sharing and compromise. It will be easier to achieve everyone's vacation goals and expectations by having advance planning sessions.

☀ *Take double the amount of accessories for the car (such as tissues, wipes, little snacks) — if you lose supplies or use more than you expected, you won't have to stop for more.*

☀ *Sometimes the most expensive mode of travel isn't, when you consider wear and tear on your nerves and the kids'. "We often use a car service or rent a car for the weekend to visit my mother, even though it's not a tremendously long train ride," says Julie Barnard. But when you look at the amount of luggage required (even for a weekend) for four people (think large teddy bears), it makes sense.*

5. Taking It Slow

Keep in mind that your normal routines will probably be topsy-turvy both as you travel and during the days at your destination. Allow enough "down" time for rest and quiet as well as for active fun. When Mary Murphy took Nicholas and Megen to Ireland, a trip that meant a lot of time spent in the car driving around the beautiful countryside (not always an interesting activity to the kids), dad Frank made sure that every day after lunch was naptime, just like at home. The kids got to sleep in the car, Mary and Frank got to see hill after hill, and when they arrived at their destination, everyone was happy. Advises Mary, "If you can keep naptimes, mealtimes, and bedtimes on the same schedule as at home, the kids will have a much easier time, and so will the parents."

⭐ When Erin and Colin Carey were small, their mother, Ruth, took them to see their grandma in Ohio. Ruth always took the red-eye —they got on the plane at 11:00 P.M. and slept until they landed. Then when they arrived, it was morning and the kids were right on their regular schedule.

⭐ Sonia Israel suggests that if there's some place you go often (a weekend home, Grandma's house), keep as much duplicate equipment there (everything from cribs to diapers and baby food) as you can.

☀ *Assign each child a number. Have a jar or container full of slips of paper with their numbers on them from which they must draw to see who will clean out the back-seat, bring in the luggage, or do odd jobs.*

☀ *Beth Yow remembers spending many traveling hours observing silly rules for car trips. For instance, every time she and her sister Laura saw a car with a burned-out headlight, they both had to scream, "Pediddle!"*

6. Giving Your Child Responsibilities

In addition to assigning a research project to your child, let him also help with the navigation. Honing map skills will only be a part of the benefit. Annie credits her dad's letting her read maps and even make some navigational decisions on a trip to Washington, D.C., when she was ten, for her lifelong fascination with geography and maps. Annie's dad was also determined to get as much written information about each destination as was available, so he sent for travel brochures for every trip the family undertook. The trick? He always put Annie's name on the return address so she received all the mail. When Annie was older, she was in charge of both mailing and keeping track of the information that arrived.

7. Avoiding Power Struggles

Avoid setting up power struggles. Be as flexible as you can. (If that means you have to scrap a planned visit to a museum because your child's energy has given out, do it!) You can reserve the important decisions for the adults, but you will find that leaving less critical decision making for the kids (even toddlers can make *some* decisions) works well for everybody. David Israel, even when he was 3 years old, was always very sure about what he would and wouldn't do. To fold him into the decision-making process for vacation planning, his parents put him in charge of when to stop for gas. David watched that gas gauge very carefully, and whenever he thought it was too close to empty, he would look for a gas station and inform whoever was driving that it was time to stop. Even when it wasn't absolutely necessary, the family would stop when informed about the low fuel. This feeling of authority and confidence that he could perform a very important task was a real "behavior enhancement."

★ *Joanne Greenberg and her sons, Aaron, Ben, and Coby, do a lot of traveling in the car. Each of the boys always wants to sit in the front seat, which has room for only one. Joanne's solution: Each of the boys takes a turn as "boy of the day": that means he gets to sit in the front seat if he wants, he gets to choose a seat in the restaurant, and so on.*

★ *Sydny Miner collects small sizes of everything: snack foods, condiments, the napkin/cutlery packs that come with take-out dinners, toys, and the Dover $1 activity/sticker/stencil books to take on family trips.*

8. Considering Family Personality

Consider the personality, habits, and interests of your family. For some families, adventure parks like Disneyland and Six Flags are the ultimate. Some prefer museums, others shopping, and still others outings to beachside resorts. Some families enjoy roughing it (while others need their showers!). The Brokaws have always been avid campers. Fortunately, all the Brokaw children grew to enjoy the outdoors as much as their parents and have continued to hone their camping skills in such diverse places as our national parks and remote areas of the Himalayas.

☀ *Now it can be told. Meredith was "The Phantom" who left treats, tiny gifts, or quarters rewarding good behavior and sad-face notes when her children's behavior wasn't up to par during a trip. It took the pressure off the parents to constantly admonish the three girls.*

☀ *When the Roberts family was in Egypt, they would get up at the crack of dawn to see the Pyramids and were back before lunch to spend the rest of the day by the pool. "It's the only sane way to travel," says mom Cokie Roberts.*

23

☀ When Remy and his friend Adam were 8 years old, they accompanied their moms to the restaurant Windows on the World at the World Trade Center in New York City to see the Statue of Liberty at sunset. The boys got to dress up and be treated like adults by the waiters and by their moms. The boys' behavior was impeccable as they sipped their Shirley Temples and toasted the sunset.

☀ Don't think your kids will be any better behaved on the road or in someone else's house than they are at home.

9. Adapting to Change

Some people adapt to change easily, others don't. Be aware of what sort you and your family are. Rested and well-fed people of all ages are much more apt to enjoy their trip. Sometimes it's easy to fall into the trap of "getting your money's worth." If your passengers need to rest, stop and take a break. "When we were single," remembers Wanda McDaniel Ruddy, "Al and I would run around like crazy seeing everything we could in one day and then drop into bed, nearly dead. But when we began traveling with John and Ali, we became much more conscious of eating regular meals and stopping to get some rest. To tell the truth, we became much happier travelers ourselves." Wanda's best recommendation? "Avoid doing too much in one day; keep both your own limitations and your children's in mind at all times."

10. Considering Children's Ages

Always remember that a child's age plays the most important part in making decisions during a trip. Plan your outings first with children in mind and then the adults. Subjecting older kids to programs for young ones, or forcing young kids to accompany older kids on more sophisticated outings, usually doesn't work for anyone. If you have kids of all ages, a good solution might be to plan a vacation where some freedom is available for older kids and supervised outings and programs are available for younger kids (resorts are perfect). Or you can make plans to spend time with the little ones while the older ones go off safely on their own.

★ Hildy Gottlieb Hill always dresses the kids in layers on the airplane, not only because they can peel according to whether they are too cold or too hot, but also because they can remove any piece of clothing that gets spilled on.

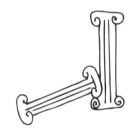

★ Cokie Roberts has always tried to take her children to ruins rather than museums. "Even when Rebecca was only 3 years old, she was fascinated by ruins because she could run around to her heart's content. She also spent a lot of time acting and dramatizing among the ruins. We once caught her pretending to sell pottery as she said, 'Pottery for sale from Athens, Delphi, and Santa Monica.'"

Tie small stuffed animals or dolls to your child's car seat so they will always be within reach.

If you are traveling with a toddler, remember to childproof your temporary quarters. The first thing to do upon reaching your destination is to check bathrooms, balconies, and furniture with sharp edges; cover electrical outlets with tape, heavy furniture, or outlet covers; secure or move objects that can be pulled off tables.

If you've got an infant/toddler, get a lightweight but sturdy traveling stroller that can fit in an overhead compartment. You can always use it for luggage and/or bears.

TODDLERS AND PRESCHOOLERS

When dealing with 2- to 5-year-olds, it is wise to take into account their self-centeredness, short attention span, and requirement for what seems like constant movement. So when you find yourself in long car rides, stop often, even if it's only for a couple of minutes, and let the kids jump up and down or run around. When planning the vacation, you may want to consider a resort where toddlers can run around and not bother anyone rather than spend long periods of time in confined spaces. Keeping this in mind, it makes sense to postpone long trips to theme parks until your child is about 4 or 5, unless pushing a stroller and waiting on lines while others go on rides is your idea of fun. This generally means no art museums, unless it's a children's museum, which can be a perfect destination for kids of all ages. (*See Resources, page 137.*)

When your child is 3, she will be thrilled with all kinds of activities, from running around to sitting and watching a movie to participating in organized arts and crafts. This is also a great age to begin negotiations, because a 3-year-old is probably a better negotiator than you are and relishes the process. This is where Annie's theory of "if you try just one bite of the taco, then we can run around the park" proves true, time and again. Just keep in mind – 3-year-olds still need their rest. Four-year-olds love to explore and can conceptualize and articulate their observations and experiences. Explaining some amazing historical facts in story form works great for this age group, as do any children's museums, children's sections or areas of special interest in a regular museum (such as a museum of natural history or science), and beach vacations (4-year-olds can spend hours pouring water from one bucket into another, making simple sand castles, and collecting shells).

SCHOOL-AGE CHILDREN

Whatever you do on vacation with school-age kids should be kid-driven. Particularly for children under 10, the high points of any vacation are often things that parents consider ordinary or quite incidental, such as going swimming every day, buying sodas from the machine in the hallway, watching TV in bed, eating breakfast out. "When the kids were little," remembers Annie, "we welcomed the fact that they had a different idea of what was fun. By doing what they considered fun with them, we all had a great time, and Gary and I remembered how much we loved doing silly, simple things together with our parents and siblings."

This is the perfect time to build a family vacation around a child's specific interest, such as dinosaurs, horses, marine life, architecture, science, different cultures, and sports. School-age children are active explorers, discoverers, inventors, experimenters — they like to get up and do, rather than sit back and watch. This is the age when involving your child in the planning and decision-making processes increases the chances that she will enjoy the trip. You will also find that trips will be very instructive in learning about family budgets, geography, map reading, and making choices, not to mention sportsmanship in game playing.

This is also the age when children begin to appreciate spending time with family. Visits to the grandparents, aunts, uncles, cousins help cement a child's sense of belonging and awareness of family. These trips can be surprisingly fun-filled adventures for the children. They'll love hearing the family stories about when their parents were little when you ask your parents to get out the toys you played with as a child. Sharing family history can be a rewarding experience for children of this age and for the adults as well.

☀ *When Lisa is looking for her mom in a crowd and really wants to get her attention, she calls her "Annie" instead of "Mom" and finds her right away.*

A school-age child is also the right age for beginning visits to amusement parks because he is able to walk long distances, tolerate the lines, and enjoy the adventure with you. Kids can now try rides that are more adventurous (and less "childish"), and they really appreciate the variety offered to them. They still have great imaginations, so they can visualize themselves as riding in space, flying an airplane, braving the rapids, and more.

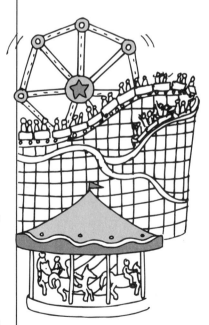

School-age children have, by this age, mastered the art of negotiation, particularly when it comes to money. This can be difficult when the family is on vacation, since there are endless tempting choices of where to spend money and on what. These decisions are always personal, but we have found that giving a child a specific amount of money (it can be as little as fifty cents) to spend at a given time in whatever way he chooses works best. Remembers Beth Yow, "When my sister and I were about 9 and 10, and we went to Great Adventure in New Jersey, Mom gave us each ten dollars to spend on things other than rides and lunch for the day. She didn't care what we bought — that was up to us. But if what we chose cost one penny more than what she had given us, we had to spend our allowance. It really taught us to choose carefully, but at the same time made us feel great that we could buy whatever we wanted!"

TEEN-AGERS

Teens, more than any other age group, need to feel that they have some control over the vacation. Giving them a real role in the decision making and letting them help with the planning results in a successful vacation. Remember, this is the age where they will also need to have some space of their own, so when it's appropriate, give them that added responsibility and freedom. If you are traveling together, allow them to choose the day's itinerary. If you are at a self-contained resort, you will find it easy for them to be quite independent and do many things on their own within a safe and protected environment. But don't think teens would prefer not to travel with their families!

In 1992, the Hyatt Hotel corporation did an interesting study on vacationing teens. They conducted a telephone survey of 500 teens (244 girls and 256 boys) ages 12 to 17 (each of whom had vacationed five days or more with at least one of their parents). The majority of these teens saw vacation as an opportunity to leave their cares behind and immerse themselves in a world of relaxation and fun, rather than as a family obligation. They actually liked to spend time with their parents. This reinforces our belief that traveling with children of any age is rewarding and memorable for all family members.

Other somewhat surprising findings:

1. What teens pack:

Ninety-three percent pack "books or magazines"; 87 percent pack their own tapes or CDs for their vacation (81 percent also pack a "portable tape or CD player"); 74 percent take cameras; 58 percent pack "sports or athletic equipment"; 39 percent pack "crossword puzzles or games," while 36 percent pack "electronic games"; 23 percent pack "art supplies." (Ages 12 to 13 are happier with "crossword puzzles or games.")

2. How do they see their family vacation experience?

Eighty-five percent say they are "happiest on vacation" where they can "unwind, shed some inhibitions and experience something new"; 93 percent are more relaxed; 82 percent are more adventurous; 76 percent are more athletic than at home. They like the fact that "families spend quality time together" (as a matter of fact, the survey found that most teens prefer family vacations to being left to their own devices at home). And there's more: 85 percent "like traveling with their parents"; 81 percent said, "My parents were very relaxed on vacation"; 76 percent would rather "go on vacation with their parents than stay home by themselves."

★ Monitor the cable TV and pay-per-view channels in your hotel, or you'll be in for some surprises when you get the bill!

★ When Joshua Gordon reached teen-age years and began traveling by himself, his main goal was to pack his own suitcase and make it as light as possible. His recommendation: a backpack with a detachable daypack. This way you can carry everything with you on airplanes, trains, and buses, but have a smaller case for day trips.

11. Dealing with Hotels; Questions to Ask

LODGING

Hotels treat children as special guests these days. Hilton, Marriott, Howard Johnson, Ritz Carleton, Four Seasons, Holiday Inn Worldwide, and Hyatt, among others, include special rates (kids stay for free), special meal rates, and children's menus (some even have room-service menus for kids), lending desks for toys, video games, and tapes, and special camps and day programs. Armin Weitzman, 8, has spent several vacations in the kids' program at the Grand Wailea Resort in Hawaii. It is his dream come true. Every day he learns about different things — about the coral reef and fish in the ocean, about recycling (he even made his own paper), how to juggle, and how to cook nutritiously (he even got his own toque and made his own pizza). The program offers games, a computer room, a mini-Olympics, crafts, videos, a soda fountain, and Armin's favorite pool and water slides. "It's the best vacation because there are so many different things to do. And my mom is always by the pool so I can find her and play with her, too. The only thing is — I never want to go home!"

Camps vary in the kinds and scope of programs and facilities they offer for children, but more and more hotels offer *some* kind of camp-like activities for kids of all ages. Call the hotel in the area where you're traveling — if one chain doesn't have what you are looking for, the next one probably will.

★ When the Robertses traveled with Rebecca and Lee, they always tried to stay in cabins rather than hotels so they could be in charge of their own meals and the kids could run around outside and no one would be disturbed.

★ Explain that the food and drinks in the mini-bar cost quite a bit of money and make your own rules regarding its use. The first time the Gilbars checked into a hotel with the kids (Marc was 3, Lisa was 8), Marc thought everything in the mini-bar was free. By the time Annie and Gary returned to the room from an adult dinner, the bar was empty (except for the liquor, of course).

★ *Tip from Susan Dolgen: "Mark your room by tying something that your child will recognize to the outer doorknob. This will give your explorer a way to find his way back."*

★ *Make some room-service rules for your family. Keep track of room-service calls (each time you order and a meal is delivered, there is an additional charge).*

★ *Some people ask that the mini-bar be cleared out before their arrival so that they can keep their own snacks refrigerated — and save on the items inside.*

Kim Marshall, director of public relations at the Grand Wailea Resort on Maui in Hawaii, helped us put together a list of questions that are helpful when deciding on a hotel for your vacation. Even if you are only planning to spend one night, you may find the information you will get quite useful. Kim suggests that you consider your own family interests in deciding which questions you need answered. For example, if you don't have any tiny tots, skip the questions about cribs or bottles. If you don't have any teens, you probably won't care about the availability of teen lounges.

On general lodging, Kim suggests asking the following:

★ Are the accommodations hotel rooms or condominium units or cottages with kitchens?
★ If they are hotel rooms: Are there connecting rooms? Is there a refrigerator in the room? Can you make any meals in the rooms? Does the room have a balcony?
★ What is the range of prices and is there a reduced rate for children? Is there a charge for a crib or roll-away bed?
★ Is there a babysitting service? Are they bonded?
★ Is there a pool? How big is it?
★ Are there special services, programs, and/or facilities for children, and what are they?

DINING

★ What type of dining areas are there?
★ Is there a children's dining room? A children's menu? Is there a dress requirement? Is there a meal plan, and if yes, is it mandatory or optional (this is applicable to a resort)?

SPECIAL SERVICES

★ Is there a supervised program?
★ If yes, what are the planned activities, and what are the ages of the children who participate?
★ Is a minimum number of children needed to participate? (There often is, and if enough kids don't sign up, it may be canceled.)
★ When is it held — time of the year, days of the week, and hours of the day?
★ What is the daily or hourly fee?
★ Is there a doctor or nurse in residence or on call? Where is the nearest hospital and pharmacy?

Kim Marshall also suggests asking a resort to send your child an event schedule before you leave on your trip. If there isn't one, it may be a sign that daily activities are not well planned.

12. Making It Familiar

Bring along familiar items from home like a child's blanket, a nightlight, stuffed animals, and the like. Have your child choose those familiar things he wants to bring and let him pack them himself to increase the feeling of familiarity and the confidence that these things that he owns and has chosen will actually be coming with him. Have a young child place his own suitcase in the car so he can see it will be with him. Explain that although he is bringing some of his favorite things, his other toys will all be there when he returns home. And before you leave the house, remember to assure your young child that you all will be coming back.

You may also find that sticking to some comforting rules that you follow at home increases your child's confidence that things won't be so strange and foreign on the trip away from home. Going to bed later than usual is fine occasionally, but you'll probably find that the kids will be overtired if they don't get enough rest. When the Yows, from Philadelphia, went on trips by car to Georgia and Cold Spring Harbor in New York, mom Sally always tried to keep the girls, Laura and Beth, to their bedtime schedules. At first, remembers Beth, "we'd resist getting to bed – we were on vacation, too. But as the trip wore on, we wore down. We got to bed, and then we were energetic and ready to go first thing in the morning (probably a lot earlier than our parents would have liked)."

★ Paul and Terry Bilsky try to stretch their home rules when they are on vacation. They might let Lee stay up a little longer, have more ice cream, or have that last swim in the pool, since he is on vacation, too!

★ Unless it's absolutely necessary (i.e., the bear/blanket your child won't go to sleep/calm down without), don't bring anything you can't replace.

13. Avoiding Backseat Terror

Ever hear the term "backseat terror"? If you haven't, you must be the only one. Every child, even the most perfect of angels, will at some time or another get a message from the secret "make your parents crazy" fairy. It is somehow inevitable, but if you are prepared to deal with your sweet Jekyll turning into the monster Hyde, all will be well. Annie's sister, Sonia Israel, has watched her sweet son, David, gleefully take on the role many times, and even turn his older and sometimes more reasonable sister, Sarah, into his accomplice.

Now that she has successfully dealt with this phenomenon more than once, Sonia advises: "Do something as soon as you hear the kids start to argue, before things get out of hand. Then, rather than cajoling or threatening your kids (it's impossible to reason with tired, irritated, fidgety children), stop the car as soon as it is safe to do so. Pull over and tell your children to get out and settle their problems and when they're done, the trip can continue. (Try to stay out of whatever the problem is. Kids always want to see whom you're going to side with, so it's best to keep quiet as much as possible.)" Just the process of getting out of their seats into the air, having some time of their own and the power to solve the situation almost always results in a solution and renewed communication.

✷ When Meredith Brokaw and her three children, aged 6, 8, and 10, were traveling from New York to South Dakota, she "gave" each child five dollars at the beginning of the trip. She taped a chart to the dashboard with each girl's name. Every time Meredith had to scold one of the girls, she got a quarter deducted from her total. When they arrived in Yankton, they got the amount of money remaining. The girls can't remember exactly how much money they had left, but Meredith remembers that nobody had five dollars.

✷ Look for detachable shades for use in your car windows while your children are napping. They keep the car cool, and the glare off, and are easily stored.

14. Building Anticipation

The miles will sail by when the kids can anticipate upcoming places, events, and experiences they will be encountering. If in two hours you will pass by the longest bridge in the world, let them know it, ask them to draw what they think it will look like, talk about bridges, etc. If tonight's dinner will be a different experience (Cajun chicken, New England clam chowder, or Mexican enchiladas), discuss what you know about the origins to heighten the anticipation. Such surprises can make the time slip away and the actual event even more enjoyable.

Also remember that one of the main reasons to take children traveling is to introduce them to what is *different* from what they have at home. Says Sharon Boorstin, a travel writer who goes all over the world with kids Adam, 10, and Julia, 15, "We want to help them realize that there is a whole world out there beyond Los Angeles. When we went to Hawaii, we asked the kids to point out all the things (plants, vistas, people) that were different from what we see back home. We also asked them to point out things that were the *same* as at home to make them feel secure."

Don't underestimate your kids' palates, even the little ones. Our friend's kids discovered fried bananas and guava jelly in Jamaica. On the other hand, don't be surprised if they refuse to eat stuff you were sure they would like.

Blake Epstein with his mom, Penny, took his first trip to Europe this past year. At 8, Blake is not a real art fan, but because he had studied the Mona Lisa in class just that year and his mom had pointed it out to him before they left home, Blake was especially thrilled to see the famous work at the Louvre in Paris.

☀ *A great gift for a child is a miniature toiletry kit that he can keep packed with travel-size products for an overnight or week-end trip. This makes it so easy to remember the small necessities like a toothbrush, toothpaste, favorite shampoo, hairbrush, and sunblock, which are so often forgotten.*

☀ *When packing the trunk of your car, place your kids' suitcases on top. They are much more inclined to need something out of their bags than you are, so having them within easy reach will make life much easier.*

☀ *Tip from Teresa Nathanson, mother of three boys and a champion packer: "Stick to simple cotton clothes. For each child, bring favorite T-shirts and shorts, a pair of sweatpants and a sweatshirt, a pair of jeans, a jacket, changes of underwear and socks, a bathing suit, a pair of sneakers, one 'dress-up' outfit, a couple of hats (one is bound to get lost, but don't bring more because you always end up buying one as a memento from the trip), sunglasses, and sunblock."*

15. Packing

Being a well-organized packer takes practice. More parental supervision may be needed in the beginning, but as children get older, their skills improve, and you will need to intervene less. Even very young children are capable of packing their own suitcases or helping you make decisions about what to pack. Start out by helping them with a list of what they will need. (If you have a home computer, let each child make his own "trip list" to keep on file; they can adapt it themselves for each trip — whether it's for a week at the beach or an overnight at a friend's house.) Then give them suggestions about additional items they might want to take (remembering to advise them that five-foot-tall teddy bears, no matter how beloved, will not travel well). Your list should include items they might not think of (dressier shoes, a nice sweater or jacket for going out to dinner, a plastic bag for dirty laundry). Eventually, they'll even make their own lists. Ronna Gordon has a rule for her three kids: "If it's not worn at home, there's not a chance they'll wear it on the trip."

Now let your children do the actual packing. This accomplishes several things. First, it gives them a sense of how to organize. Second, it gives them a good feeling to be "in charge" of such an important activity.

You may want to buy your child his own soft-sided suitcase. They are inexpensive and can be squashed down to fit into any space. They are also lightweight so the kids can carry their own luggage. Many stores and catalogues now personalize such luggage for a nominal charge. Gary Gilbar's method was to give each child a duffel bag in a different color and tape a stripe of masking tape in a contrasting color in a diagonal across one side. He also marked each bag with the owner's name tag. This makes spotting the suitcases at the airport, in the back of the van, or in the hotel lobby very easy.

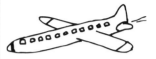

⭐ If you arrive in time to board the plane early, ask the pilot if the children can visit the cockpit.

⭐ Flight attendants, especially on a full flight, won't be able to help out too much in keeping your children occupied. If they're not harried and seem to like kids, enlist their help. Otherwise, the more you can do for yourself, the better: carry self-heating bottle packs, serve baby food at room temperature, and have plenty of activities.

16. Traveling by Airplane

Today, flying to and from a destination is more and more common. Airlines have established many services and guidelines for traveling with children, recognizing that families with children are big business and that kids' needs must be considered. Heeding some advice on flying with kids will make your flight more enjoyable. The given in this situation is that flying with children over the age of 4 has become easier and easier. Kids with their Penny Whistle backpacks (*see page 51*) will have more than enough to keep them busy and in their seats, and an in-flight movie (if the kids are interested) can take care of nearly two hours of time.

Flying with infants and 2- and 3-year-olds can be more complicated. Children this age require a lot more equipment, and that can be cumbersome. It is also difficult to keep 2- and 3-year-olds occupied in their seats for long periods of time. Flying is not the ideal way to travel with toddlers, but if you must, here are some hints to make the experience as painless and as enjoyable as possible:

★ Make sure each child has his own carry-on activity pack. *(See The Penny Whistle Travel Backpack, page 51.)*

★ Order a child's meal at least twenty-four hours before the flight. Choices range from hot dogs and hamburgers to chicken nuggets and macaroni and cheese. Airlines always have plenty of juice along, but if your child just loves those juices in a box (complete with a straw), pack a couple in his backpack.

★ If you can, arrange to sit in the bulkhead seats. These are seats in the beginning of a row with no seats in front of them. This gives you added room to put a bassinet or to have your toddler sit and draw when it is safe to do so.

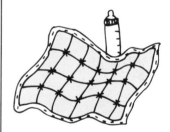

⭐ It's not a bad idea to carry a small lightweight blanket. Planes can get chilly and there are never enough blankets to go around.

⭐ When purchasing your airline tickets remember that accompanied kids (ages 2 through 11) receive 25 percent off normal coach fares when they sit in their own seat. Check for special children's fares and advance-purchase fares.

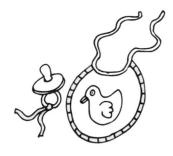

★ Try to get up and walk around the plane with your child at least once every half an hour; it's good for everyone. You can even do some of our stretch exercises in the back of the plane without disturbing anyone. But please don't let your child march up and down the aisles by himself — it is dangerous, and annoying to the other passengers and to cabin attendants who are busy working in the aisles.

★ Because airplane travel can seem so long, the inevitable question "Are we almost there?" will be asked. To put the time span in perspective, tell your child, in terms she can understand, how far you have to go — for example, explain that you'll get there in one hour, which is as long as her favorite cartoon show.

★ If you are taking a baby on a plane, dress him warmly in layers because airplanes do get cold. Make sure all children carry an extra sweater or jacket.

★ Ask the airline representative (or your travel agent) if your airline offers bassinets and/or car seats. It's easier to use theirs than to carry your own.

★ Takeoff and landing can sometimes be hard on a child's ears. Talk to your pediatrician. Dr. Peter Waldstein (our advisor on *The Penny Whistle Sick-in-Bed Book*) suggests that giving an infant a pacifier or a bottle for both takeoff and landing will help prevent pain in the ears from changes in cabin pressure. Older kids can chew gum or suck hard candy. You may also ask your doctor about giving an antihistamine to your children.

★ Children and adults should drink a lot of water and/or juice on an airplane to prevent dehydration. Coffee, tea, and soda containing caffeine should be avoided. This can mean more trips to the bathroom; you'll just have to resign yourself to navigating those aisles to the back bathrooms more than once. (Think of it as exercise.)

★ Some people prefer taking night flights with children (these usually leave around 10 P.M.). They can be effective for very young children because their body clock tells them to sleep anyway.

PENNY WHISTLE RULES OF THE ROAD

CHILDREN TRAVELING ALONE

You can write to the National Child Safety Council and ask for a copy of their booklet "Kids and Teens in Flight," Office of Consumer Affairs, Dept. of Transportation, 400 7th Street S.W., Washington, DC 20590. The booklet *When Kids Fly* is available free from Massport, Ten Park Plaza, Boston, MA 02116-3971.

No child under the age of 5 can travel alone. A child can travel alone unsupervised from the ages of 5 to 12 only on direct, nonstop flights. If a child is over 11, he won't be supervised, although unaccompanied children ages 12 to 15 can receive assistance on connecting flights if you request it and make the appropriate arrangements with the airlines. Make sure he knows what to do in an emergency.

Airline officials urge parents to get to the airport early when a child is flying alone, so there is plenty of time for all the paperwork. Be sure to have on hand the name, address, and phone numbers of the person who is to pick up your child at the other end.

It is the airline's priority to get your child from your hands to his destination, not to entertain him along the way. Make it clear to your child that the stewardess is not his babysitter and he has to entertain himself.

Some airlines are prepared for kids with game books, miniature pilot's pins, a deck of cards, and so on. Always ask, because flight attendants are often busy and may forget to bring these materials to your child. Some airlines have special clubs for kids that offer benefits like a children's magazine, a deck of cards, a pen, or an activity book.

If your child has never been on an airplane and is traveling alone, visit your local airport before the day of departure. Arrange for him to meet some airline personnel. They are usually very friendly and eager to talk to kids about airplanes and air travel.

Teen flyers can undertake more responsibility when they fly alone. Here are some tips on teens flying solo:

★ Make sure your teen-ager has enough cash to cover incidentals like gum, magazines, and telephone calls.

★ Make sure he knows how to call collect, or give him your telephone credit card number.

★ Make sure he has a copy of his itinerary within easy reach.

★ Make sure he has a telephone number where you (or any other live person, as opposed to an answering machine) can be reached.

★ Tell your teen that he shouldn't be shy about asking airlines personnel for help, and if he doesn't receive it, he should ask to see the supervisor on duty. Kids are sometimes reluctant to ask for help and need to be reassured that it's O.K. to do so.

★ Instruct your teen *never* to leave the airport should his flight be delayed.

★ Remind your child *never* to leave the airport with a stranger.

★ *Amtrak allows children to ride unaccompanied only during the day and on trips with no changes. The child must be 8 years or over. If children are between the ages of 8 and 11, they must be interviewed to see if they are mature enough to make the trip.*

★ *Greyhound and Trailways allow children 5 years old and older to ride unaccompanied by an adult — but only in the daytime. The bus driver is responsible for the child.*

☀ *If you are caravaning, take walkie-talkies with you for communicating between cars.*

☀ *When Annie was 8, her parents took her to Athens. The trip was full of visits to museums and people's homes, but what Annie remembers to this day is sitting on a stone in the Parthenon, feeling very small in the surrounding ruins, and then getting to run around the rest of the visit.*

17. Traveling by Car and Train

Most of us will get to our vacation destinations by car. Much of that time will be spent playing games, and we have included an entire section of games for all ages to play together in the car *(see pages 55)*. We have also included many recipes for what we call "road food" — snacks kids can eat in the car that are nutritious, delicious, and not messy or perishable *(see pages 113)*.

Here are some additional thoughts about dealing with car travel:

★ You may find that rotating seats in the car every now and then gives everyone a different perspective on sights and a feeling that no one family member is more important than another. (That seat next to the driver does have the aura of authority, doesn't it?)

★ When the kids begin to fight, stop the car and let them have a break (*(see pages 32 for additional thoughts on dealing with irritable kids)*. You may also decide to change the seating arrangement as a solution.

★ Never break this rule: The car does not move unless the kids are in their car seats or seat belts. (Lisa Gilbar for years believed that cars just don't start unless the seat belt is attached to its holster!) Seat belts save lives and as a result, in most states, driving without a seat belt is *illegal* and carries a hefty fine. For all these reasons we repeat: *Never start the car unless everyone is wearing a seat belt and young kids are strapped in their car seats!*

★ As you are traveling, keep the kids informed of your plans. Tell them where you are going, what you want to see, how you will get there. Play the games on your map *(see page 63)* so they will see where they are headed. Not only will your children find this interesting, but it also helps to give them a sense of security.

PENNY WHISTLE

★ It helps some families to make a driving schedule that fits their habits. If you prefer to drive at night, so that your children can sleep during the ride, do so if you won't get too tired. If you can plan your trip so that you drive only in the mornings and then sightsee or play in the afternoons, that is a terrific option. If you must drive for long stretches, at least try to break the trip into intervals so that everyone can get out and stretch even for a couple of minutes. Says our friend Julie Shapiro, "It's better to get somewhere later with a smile than on time in tears."

★ Sometimes "awards" are the solution. Annie's sister, Sonia, has long been a champion of stickers. Her kids have gotten many sticker awards for any milestones, such as the first hundred miles traveled, the end of the first day, no arguments in a whole day (or at least an hour), and so on.

★ Traveling by train is very similar to taking trips by car, except that you can move around more easily and frequently. Train travel is also more leisurely. Try taking a short train trip to a destination not far from your home. Trains hold a fascination for people of all ages and the kids will really love this treat! This is especially wise if you are planning to take a long train ride — you want to be sure that everyone loves the experience as much as you do. The same backpacks and boxes can be used on the train as in the car. Be sure to also take along something to eat and drink. There are no refrigerators, and the food available on trains varies greatly in quantity, variety, and quality.

☀ *Jill and Remy often take the train from Boston to New York. When Remy was young, they would plan their picnic lunch, and a special toy (with lots of pieces to put together) was purchased to be opened on the train. Jill wasn't tired from driving and she and Remy had spent many fun hours being together.*

☀ *Motion sickness is a result of the inner ear (which governs balance) sensing that a vehicle is moving, while the eyes, which are focused inside the car, are sending a signal that you are sitting still. The solution is to encourage children to focus their eyes on distant objects out the front (not the side) window. Front seats are easier on carsick-prone children than backseats because they can more easily focus on the horizon from the front. Also, avoid eating heavy meals and have fresh air circulating through the car*

R A I L · W A Y S

18. Sightseeing

Obviously, sightseeing is going to be a large part of your trip, possibly the reason you are going to a new place. Look for spots your children will like, rest frequently, and reserve time for spontaneous plans. Allow time for relaxation. An unhurried vacation is a successful one.

★ In addition, it is really important not to deflate the things your children find exciting and wonderful. Try to turn their attention to what you feel is a more important aspect of what you are seeing, but understand that what is fascinating to your child may not seem important or unusual to you, and what appeals to parents may not always be appreciated by the children.

★ Children are fascinated by the obvious differences between the lives they are seeing and life back at home — the houses people live in, the forms of transportation, the way people dress, the local customs, the foods they eat.

★ Parents sometimes are astonished at personality changes on their trips. Normally outgoing, assertive kids can become quite shy and dependent around strangers and in unconventional and alien surroundings (and vice versa). Keep in mind that once they return to more familiar turf, their usual personalities will return as well.

★ Sightseeing is sometimes synonymous with shopping, especially after you have seen the museum or ruins or countryside. A good way to control spending and teach some money values is to give each child a certain amount of money at the beginning of each day, or of the trip, and allow him to decide how it's going to be spent. Parents won't always agree with the spending decisions, but learning how to spend allowances does take practice and should improve in time!

★ Bring along the brochures, books, and magazines you collected before embarking. Taking the time to learn about what you are seeing and asking questions will enhance the trip for everyone.

★ When Annie and Gary traveled to France with the kids, their program was always the same. They did their sightseeing for only a couple of hours in the morning, spent each afternoon at the beach where the kids did anything they pleased, and then walked around the town in the evening. In this way, the kids were always prepared for and excited about the next day's adventurous sights, because they knew that in the afternoon they would always get to just play. Some afternoons the kids got to choose a new place to go, and it was always a child's kind of destination. More than once it was the same amusement park in Antibes, where the kids went on the same rides over and over again. For them, it was paradise!

★ When the kids seem suddenly cranky or when they begin to dawdle, it's time to stop sightseeing. Kids can absorb only so much information. When they are "full," it's time to relax and play. If you keep this in mind and tell them, "You seem tired — let's stop, rest a bit, and then just play," they will trust you and look forward to sightseeing the next day instead of dreading what they will see as yet another "boring" excursion.

★ *If you are going to be in a crowded location, give your child a whistle on a string to hang around his neck in case of emergency. Also, dress your children in brightly colored clothing so they stand out in a crowd.*

★ *Before setting off for a day of sightseeing, form your own rules about what your child should do in case he gets lost or separated from your family or traveling group. Your child should know the name of the place you are staying, as well as other points of identification.*

★ *When sightseeing with kids, resist the impulse to buy the first souvenirs you see. Explain to the kids that there will be many chances to see the same things again and again, and make a game out of seeing who is the first to spot the things you see in every stand. Only when you have "cased" the area will it be time to "spot the loot" that you really want.*

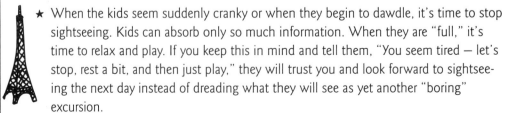

19. Going to Restaurants with Kids

All trips are likely to include eating out at least once. Eating in restaurants can be a tricky proposition. Here are some hints to help:

★ Do not choose a formal restaurant. Kids are much more comfortable in casual places, and casual places are much more comfortable with kids. It is unfair to expect young children to sit still for long periods of time surrounded by stuffy waiters carrying crystal and silver. If you don't put your kids in this position, both the kids and the restaurants will thank you.

★ If the food is slow in coming, take the kids outside for a while rather than insisting on good behavior.

★ Some parents find that if they sit next to them, their children will behave better.

★ Always ask for a children's menu. If one is not available, ask for a half order.

★ Check out the menu before you sit down in a restaurant so you'll be sure that there is something that the kids will eat.

★ It is not a great idea to order foods for your children that they normally don't like just because that's all there is on the menu. If they don't eat it at home, they won't eat it now. If you find yourself in the position of facing a menu that has nothing your kids will eat, improvise. For a long time when one of our kids was little, she would only eat pizza, macaroni and cheese, or grilled cheese. Period. But we also found that there are many accommodating chefs who can make a grilled cheese sandwich, or plain pasta with butter and cheese. It was always the preferable solution to ordering baked bass in shrimp sauce, which would have gone untouched.

★ Ask for your child's meal to be served with your appetizer so he doesn't have to wait. You can also ask for crudités (carrots and celery sticks, cucumber slices and raw radishes) to keep young mouths fed while the meal is being cooked. Most kids assume that all the crackers and rolls placed on the table were meant for them anyway.

★ You can't expect kids to wait in line or to sit for hours in a restaurant after being cooped up in a car or out sightseeing all day. To prevent a restaurant disaster, choose a place that offers fast service and simple food.

★ *Tip from Marshall Schulman: When dining out with the little ones, get something in their stomachs right away —crackers, a roll, and the like.*

★ *Annie is always in a hurry. Whenever she eats at a restaurant, she tries to guess how long it will take for her food to come.*

★ *Jake and David Gilbar take turns picking out restaurants for each meal when traveling. To their parents' delight, it's always Italian, Indian, Italian, Indian, Italian, Indian.*

20. Ending the Day Happily

It's the end of the day, and everyone is excited, but also tired. This is a good time to leave some part of the day for doing nothing — rest, taking in the atmosphere. After traveling for a whole day, try letting the children choose the evening's activities. There's nothing wrong with reading, watching a movie, playing a quiet favorite board game, or writing in a journal. (*Don't forget our End-of-the-Day Box, on page 54!*)

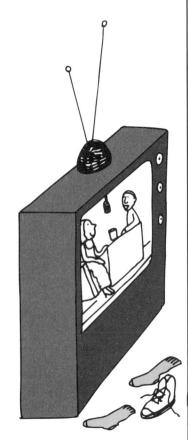

☀ *On the road, try to stay at a hotel/motel with a pool or playground. Stop early enough in the day (4:30 to 5:00) so everyone can cool out before dinner. Some places have a special playroom with a counselor where the kids can play while you relax.*

Before Leaving Home

⭐ *Children can be enrolled in frequent flyer programs, too. Check with your airline.*

UNITED STATES OF AMERICA

101234

PASSPORT

Type
P

MINER
Given Names

JONATHAN FREDERIK
Nationality

UNITED STATES OF AMERICA

Date of birth   Sex
8 APRIL 87   M

Address   Phone: (251) 123-4567
1452 PENNY WHISTLE LANE, SMALLTOWN NH 03009

PLACE PHOTO HERE

PASSPORT

DRAW AND COLOR YOUR COVER

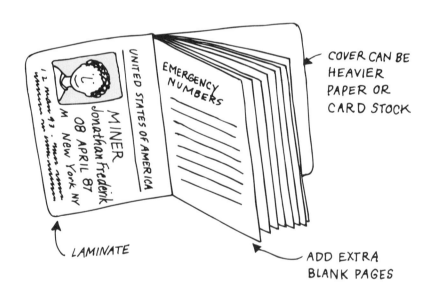

COVER CAN BE HEAVIER PAPER OR CARD STOCK

LAMINATE

ADD EXTRA BLANK PAGES

Make Your Own Passport

Photocopy the passport above and fill in the necessary information. Add a photo or drawing of your child or make your own. Include an emergency number. Color in the front of the passport with bright markers. Add extra blank pages in the back for kids to write, draw, and put stamps of where they've been. Laminate, staple pages together, and fold over. Your child can carry his passport in his backpack. It looks very official and young kids love it. It is also a valuable piece of information in case your child gets lost.

Make Your Own Postcards

It's easy to buy postcards at every stop on your trip — and useful, too, because they let your friends know where you are and what you are doing. If you send them home or collect them for yourself, they will compile a wonderful picture diary of your trip and will help your child remember where he was and what he saw.

PHOTO CARD

Another way to send postcards is to use your own photographs that you or your child has taken. Choose one such favorite shot that you have had developed at a one-hour shop and write your message on the back. Mail it just as you would a store-bought card.

⭐ Postcards are great collectibles on a trip. Lisa and Marc buy one postcard at each stop and write the day's diary on the back. These fit into photo albums with plastic dividers so you can see the front and back.

⭐ When Annie was 10, she went on her first train trip, from Geneva to Paris. Her mom packed a bag with a lunch, but at the last minute decided that it would be a treat to eat in the main dining room. Many years later, Annie still remembers that special day, when lunch was served by waiters in uniforms on a white tablecloth. She felt like a very special child!

Grandma,
wish you were here
♡ xx
love,
Remy

POST CARD

THE SECRET POSTCARD FOR OUR STAR TRAVELER

To encourage your children to write to family and friends, here is a postcard stencil that makes their messages secret to all but the receiver. Just photocopy our stencil, make several, and give them out to those who will receive your confidential cryptic messages.

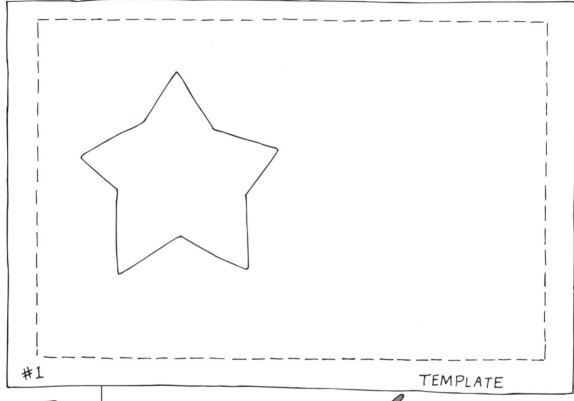

#1   TEMPLATE

GLUE TEMPLATE
ONTO CARDBOARD.

CUT OUT POSTCARD.

CUT STAR OUT OF BOTH SHEETS.

SAVE BOTH
PIECES.

Making Your Secret Grid:

1. Photocopy drawing #1 and glue to foamboard or heavy cardboard (cardboard sheets found in shirts from the laundry are perfect).
2. Cut around the dotted line as marked.
3. Cut out the star. (It's easier to cut with a knife, but that should be done by an adult.) Save all the pieces.

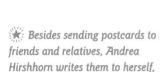

Besides sending postcards to friends and relatives, Andrea Hirshhorn writes them to herself, so when she gets home she has a ready-made diary waiting for her.

Writing Your Secret Letter from the Star Traveler (that's you):

When you put your star template over the words (see below), they form your real, secret message. The words on the outside of the star are to fool anyone who tries to read your secret code. Write these on the outside of the star.

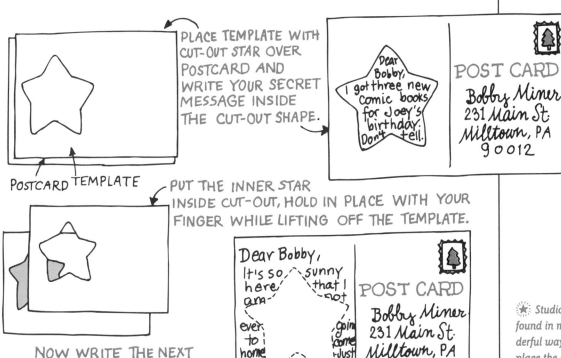

POSTCARD TEMPLATE

PLACE TEMPLATE WITH CUT-OUT STAR OVER POSTCARD AND WRITE YOUR SECRET MESSAGE INSIDE THE CUT-OUT SHAPE.

PUT THE INNER STAR INSIDE CUT-OUT, HOLD IN PLACE WITH YOUR FINGER WHILE LIFTING OFF THE TEMPLATE.

NOW WRITE THE NEXT MESSAGE ON THE OUTSIDE OF THE STAR.

Studio Tac, which can be found in most art stores, is a wonderful way of pasting. Simply place the item on top of a piece of Studio Tac paper and rub. Now the item has a sticky back and is ready to position.

To Read the Secret Message:

Your receiver holds the open star template over the postcard and your secret message appears within the borders of the star!

The Penny Whistle Travel Certificate

Just photocopy our certificate to award your child at the end of a trip *(see page 159)*. You can personalize the certificate to meet your desires — you can award one for best behavior on a trip, most adventurous traveler, most courteous-to-waitresses traveler, etc.

☀ *Before taking a trip, look through travel magazines. They often have a section on traveling with children and are great resources for well-researched travel tips and suggestions. Also, the magazines rate things so you know what you can expect from vacation spots, parks, restaurants, hotels, and packaged tours.*

☀ *Lorrie Goddard always carries an assortment of balls in the car when traveling with 2-year-old Chelsea from Los Angeles to see her family in Texas. Sometimes she even includes a small beach ball — just the act of blowing the ball up and then letting the air out keeps Chelsea busy and happy.*

Certificate of Excellence

⭐ Marc Gilbar ⭐

receives this award for making up the most & the best songs from L.A. to Portland, Oregon 🎵

Annie Gilbar
MOM

Gary Gilbar
DAD

DATE: July 12, 1994

Lisa Gilbar
SISTER:

The Penny Whistle Travel Box

To make life easier on the road, pack the following items in our Penny Whistle Box. Just about anything you will need to make sure your kids are occupied is in this box. Take it on the airplane or in the car, or put the items in a large backpack. Add some things of your choice as gift surprises for the kids — wrap them in gift paper. (Remember to hide away extra gifts for the trip home.)

For car trips and for some airplane trips, you may want to include small snack items. This will ensure that your children are not asking for food every two minutes in the car. And on the airplane, your child's hunger schedule will surely not be on the same timetable as the airline's food service, so having small "road food" snacks available will make your trip a lot happier.

It goes without saying that *The Penny Whistle Traveling with Kids Book* should be in each box or backpack so the kids will have the games at their fingertips.

☀ *For young children, include finger puppets in their travel box. They will enjoy performing their own puppet shows, or you can use them as a diversion when they are very tired or bored.*

★ *Jan Levine always packs grab bags with wrapped toys. The wrapping adds to the excitement and they take extra time to open.*

COMPASS

MAPS & GUIDEBOOKS

BATTERIES

STAMPS

STATIONERY & POSTCARDS

ADDRESSES & ADDRESS BOOK

DISPOSABLE CAMERA OR FILM FOR YOUR OWN

BLANK AUDIO CASSETTES FOR AUDIO RECORDER

BLANK VIDEO CASSETTES FOR VIDEO RECORDER

TIMER (*FOR GAMES, SEE PAGE 55*)

ACTIVITY & GAME BOOKS (*SEE RESOURCES, PAGE 137*)

LAMINATED GAMES (*SEE PAGE 56*), DRY-BOARD MARKERS, & ERASER

TRAVEL GAMES (*SEE PAGE 92*)

STICKERS

YES-&-NO BOOKS

BALLPOINT PENS

CRAYONS

PHOTO ALBUM

SPONGE BALLS, SOFT FRISBEE, JUMP ROPE, BALL, CHALK FOR PLAYGROUND STOPS (*SEE PAGE 101*)

NOTEBOOKS

PAPER

GLUE STICKS & DRAWING TOOLS

WASHABLE MARKERS

RUBBER STAMPS & STAMP PADS

MAGIC TRICKS

DICE

BOOKS ON TAPE, MUSIC & SING-ALONG TAPES

BRAINTEASER BOOKS

DOT-TO-DOT BOOKS

The Penny Whistle Travel Backpack

This is for your child to pack himself. He can pack anything he wants but he must be able to carry it himself.

These are suggestions:

HOLE PUNCH & NOTEBOOK FOR KEEPING POSTCARDS & BROCHURES

CAMERA

NOTEBOOK WITH RECLOSABLE PLASTIC BAGS FOR LITTLE ITEMS SUCH AS ADMISSION TICKETS, MATCHBOOK COVERS, & OTHER MEMENTOS

PILLOW

BOOKS TO READ

ART SUPPLIES

PAPER

FAVORITE STUFFED ANIMAL OR DOLL

SWEATSHIRT

SUNGLASSES

HAT

TRAVEL ALARM CLOCK

TOILETRY KIT

WALKMAN & FAVORITE BOOKS ON TAPE & MUSIC TAPES

A FANNY PACK (TO WEAR DURING THE DAY AS A GOOD PLACE TO HOLD COLLECTIBLES, SPENDING MONEY, ID, & EMERGENCY NUMBERS)

NOTEBOOKS

PORTABLE WORK SPACE (A CLIPBOARD WITH A PLASTIC PENCIL CASE FILLED WITH CRAYONS & COLORED PENCILS TIED ON)

★ Jan Sargeant suggests including Scotch tape in your kit for car or plane travel. Small children love to wrap tape around their fingers and attempt to pick up small items.

★ Not only are trial-size cosmetics and other sundries convenient but children love things that are miniatures of any type.

★ Airplane carry-on luggage should be geared to your kids' needs: extra change of clothes, stuffed animal, diapers and diapering gear if necessary (more than you think you'll need), books, audio tapes, paper and washable markers/crayons, even Play-Doh (if it's age-appropriate).

The Penny Whistle Tot Backpack

Useful beyond belief, this little backpack that your tot is probably used to toting to nursery school will carry all his cherished possessions. Don't fill it with necessary items like clothing and toothbrushes — add those to your own backpack or suitcases. This Tot Backpack should be full of your child's familiar and favorite things — games, small stuffed animals, cloth books, crayons, a small ball, a miniature laminated board game. This is their treasure chest to keep them occupied and smiling both on moving vehicles and at rest stops (waitresses will be forever grateful).

⭐ *Pack what you need: You can find disposable diapers almost anywhere in the U.S. (though not necessarily when you need them); you don't need to bring two weeks' supply with you.*

⭐ *Small children like to identify shapes. Cut various shapes and store them in an envelope or in a plastic travel soap box. Have them close their eyes and figure out what shape they are holding.*

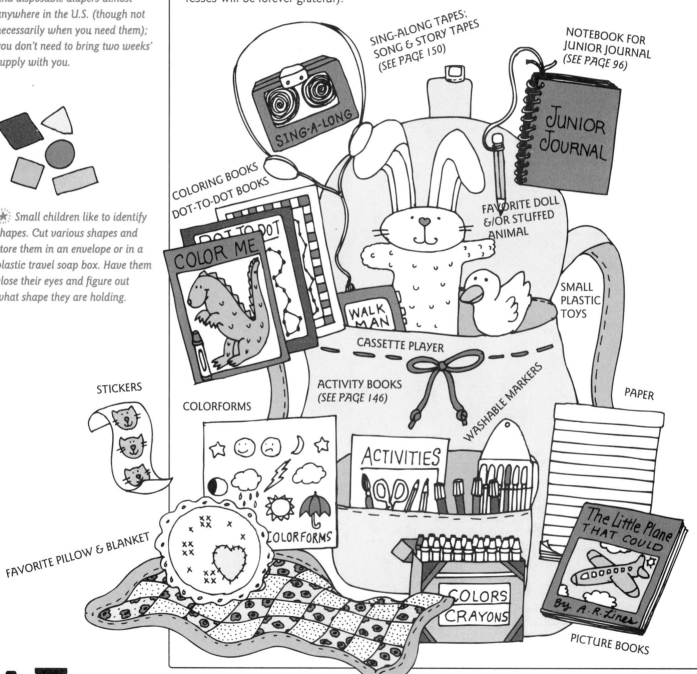

SING-ALONG TAPES; SONG & STORY TAPES (SEE PAGE 150)

NOTEBOOK FOR JUNIOR JOURNAL (SEE PAGE 96)

JUNIOR JOURNAL

SING-A-LONG

COLORING BOOKS DOT-TO-DOT BOOKS

DOT TO DOT

COLOR ME

FAVORITE DOLL &/OR STUFFED ANIMAL

WALK MAN

CASSETTE PLAYER

SMALL PLASTIC TOYS

ACTIVITY BOOKS (SEE PAGE 146)

WASHABLE MARKERS

PAPER

STICKERS

COLORFORMS

ACTIVITIES

COLORFORMS

FAVORITE PILLOW & BLANKET

COLORS CRAYONS

The Little Plane THAT COULD

BY A.R. Lines

PICTURE BOOKS

The Penny Whistle Travel First-Aid Kit

Why not pack the first-aid kit in a child's lunch box? It makes it easily visible and retrievable and you won't forget it as you take it from place to place. Use travel-size products where available. Make sure that you have necessary prescriptions for family members.

BAND-AIDS

GAUZE

COTTON BALLS

Q-TIPS

THERMOMETER

TWEEZERS

SOAP

SAFETY PINS

HYDROGEN PEROXIDE IN A PLASTIC BOTTLE

ROUTINE MEDICINES FOR MOTION SICKNESS, HEADACHES, DIARRHEA, NAUSEA

ANTIBACTERIAL CREAM

SUNBLOCK

ANY PRESCRIPTION MEDICINES

A FIRST-AID MANUAL

IPECAC SYRUP (TO INDUCE VOMITING IN CASE OF ACCIDENTAL POISONING)

ALLERGY MEDICATIONS

TISSUES

WET WIPES

INSECT REPELLENT

CALAMINE LOTION

DECONGESTANT

THROAT LOZENGES

VITAMINS

FLASHLIGHT & EXTRA BATTERIES

SCISSORS

SWISS ARMY KNIFE

LIP BALM

KAOLIN PREPARATION (LIKE PEPTO-BISMOL)

SEWING KIT

☀ *Remember to pack your health insurance identification card.*

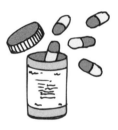

☀ *Take pediatric acetaminophen (or an appropriate substitute) on the plane in case of earache. Make sure you've got copies of your kids' prescriptions if necessary.*

☀ *Whenever Annie's dad would travel abroad he would buy foreign toiletries — Band-Aids and toothpaste from France, soap from Italy, shampoo and shaving supplies from London. When he returned home, he gave them to the kids, who thought it very sophisticated to use such foreign products.*

The Penny Whistle End-of-the-Day Box

This is to be used at the hotel, someone's home, and the like, as a diversionary addition to the other boxes and/or backpacks so the kids won't get bored with their backpack.

☆ When the Jaegers and the Webers went to Washington, D.C. for a weekend of sightseeing, they stopped at the local market to stock up on the kids' favorite snacks. It made the time between returning to the hotel and having dinner much more pleasant.

☆ Says Mary Murphy, "We always pack a bathing suit for each child, no matter where we are going. There is always a motel with an indoor or outdoor pool or a public park with a pool or a lake. Swimming is the best way for the kids to exercise and let off excess energy after sitting for long periods of time."

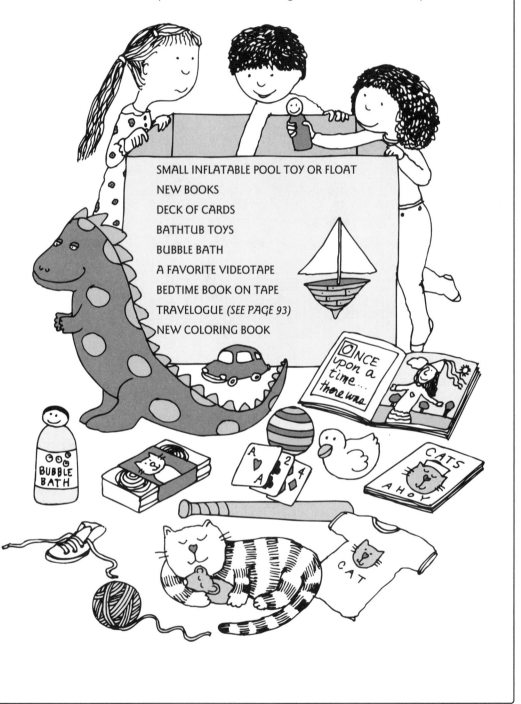

SMALL INFLATABLE POOL TOY OR FLOAT

NEW BOOKS

DECK OF CARDS

BATHTUB TOYS

BUBBLE BATH

A FAVORITE VIDEOTAPE

BEDTIME BOOK ON TAPE

TRAVELOGUE (SEE PAGE 93)

NEW COLORING BOOK

Games for Traveling

☀ *Don't forget your binoculars! Your child will enjoy using them at sights along the way but also for license-plate spotting.*

EVERY PARENT KNOWS THAT:

Children in a confined space + a long period of time = territorial disputes and innumerable squabbles caused by real or imagined indignities!

THE SOLUTION? Keep young minds and hands busy playing games.

The handy thing about these Penny Whistle games is that you can carry this book around with you since most of the games don't need any tools. You can play them wherever you are, though usually complicated spelling and writing games work better in a hotel room than inside a car.

At the end of the chapter is a list of favorite travel games you can buy at most toy and travel stores. They are all miniature and many of them are also magnetic for easy playing in a car or an airplane.

Laminated Games

☀ *Even if you bring* The Penny Whistle Traveling with Kids Book *with you on your journey, you should make photocopies of games and projects for your kids before you leave home.*

We have found that some of the best games are the ones that you want to play over and over again. When these are writing games or games where things have to be marked, you end up accumulating and using a lot of paper. This doesn't work too well in a car or airplane. Our solution is to laminate certain game cards, making it possible to reuse them. All you need are dry-board markers and an eraser. Laminating has become much more accessible, so you'll find it easy and inexpensive to laminate a few of the game cards you choose. Many copy, stationery, and hardware stores now offer laminating services. Although the costs vary, you can expect to laminate one 6-by-6-inch-square card for about $2.

Before you head off on your trip you might like to laminate

- ★ Our map of the United States
- ★ Map of your own trip
- ★ Bingo cards *(see page 58)*
- ★ Road signs *(see page 61)*
- ★ Lost & Found *(see page 60)*
- ★ Vacation *(see page 62)*

DRAW YOUR
STATE FLAG

ALASKA

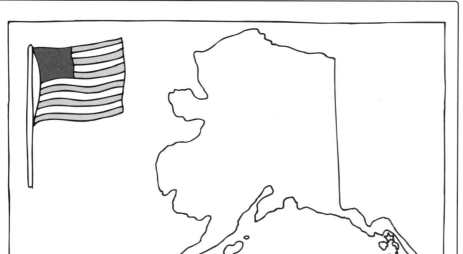

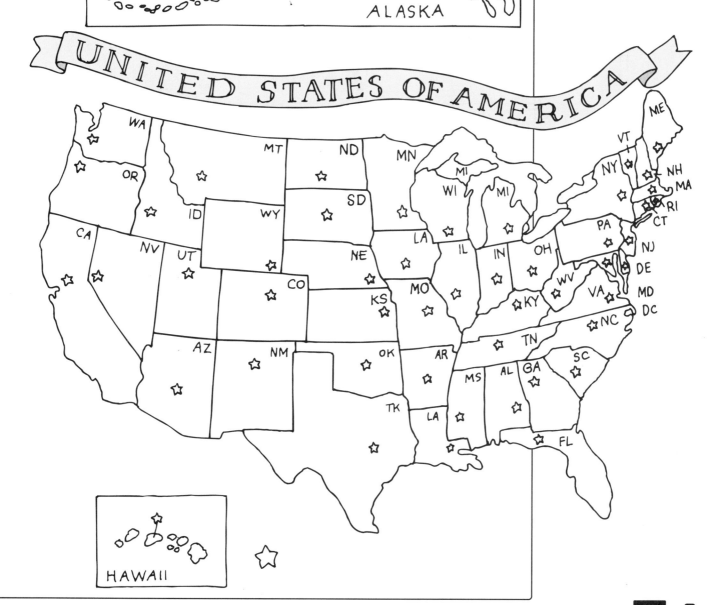

UNITED STATES OF AMERICA

WA
OR
ID
CA
NV
UT
AZ
NM
MT
WY
CO
ND
SD
NE
KS
OK
TK
MN
LA
MO
AR
LA
WI
MI
MI
IL
IN
KY
TN
MS
AL
GA
FL
OH
WV
VA
NC
SC
PA
NY
VT
ME
NH
MA
RI
CT
NJ
DE
MD
DC

HAWAII

⭐ *Joel Bennett's mom, Irene, is a champion planner of children's activities and contingencies. Irene's first stop before any trip is at the local stationery store in Skokie, Illinois, to load up on stickers. The kids use them to illustrate stories they write along the way and also to play homemade bingo.*

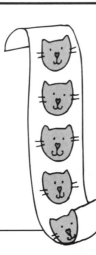

BINGO CARD

LOST & FOUND

Photocopy these lists of things to find, or make up your own as you travel. Laminate, if you'd like, for your backpack. Items in the LOST column are things that a car, hotel, or airplane might be without. Items in the FOUND column are things a car, hotel, or airplane might have. When you are traveling, choose the appropriate list for either the car, train, or hotel. Look at your environment and try to locate the "lost" and "found" items on the list. You may play alone or split the lists up between two players. Try to make up your own lists, too.

C A R	
LOST	**FOUND**
LICENSE PLATE	LUGGAGE RACK
TIRE	TRAILER
ANTENNA	BUMPER STICKERS
REAR LIGHT	POLICEMAN
PASSENGERS	A TIRE ON THE BACK
A CHILD	COLLEGE STICKER
A TOP	A DENT
TWO DOORS	BROKEN LIGHT
TRUNK	SHADE
DRIVER	DOG

☀ *Leave extra time in your schedule in case your child falls in love with a special activity. When Marc Gilbar visited the Exploratorium in San Francisco, a trip that was scheduled to last for an hour turned into three because Marc was so fascinated with the hundreds of experiments and projects there. Even three hours were not sufficient for Marc to try everything, so the Gilbars promised to return.*

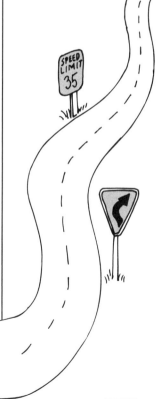

★ *Tie a shoebag to the front seat headrest so your child can reach small items himself without asking you for them.*

★ *As you walk with kids in new cities, watch for street performers. Kids love the spontaneity and talent of mimes, musicians, actors, and magicians. Such performances often have greater fascination and enjoyment for kids than sitting for hours in a seat in a concert hall.*

HOTEL

LOST	FOUND
SWIMMING POOL	BELLBOY WITH GLASSES
ROOM SERVICE	FIRE EXTINGUISHER
RADIO	ICE MACHINE
BELLBOY WITHOUT HAT	BABY WITH A BOTTLE
UNDERGROUND GARAGE	CHILDREN'S MENU
HAIR DRYER	DAY CAMP
AN OUTDOOR STAIRCASE	"NO VACANCY" SIGN
PETS	PLASTIC CUPS
"DO NOT DISTURB" SIGN	MAN IN BERMUDA SHORTS
ONE LETTER IN NEON SIGN NOT WORKING	LUGGAGE DOLLY

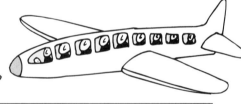

PLANE

LOST	FOUND
STEWARDESS WITH NO EARRINGS	MALE STEWARD
COFFEE WITH NO MILK	MAN WEARING A HAT
BAREFOOT PASSENGER	TELEPHONE
PILOT WITHOUT HAT	BABY
BROKEN "SEAT BELT" SIGN	MAN WITH MUSTACHE
"NO SMOKING" SIGN	STROLLER
AIRSICKNESS BAG	RED BACKPACK
SAFETY VIDEO	COMEDY STATION ON RADIO
MOVIE	ORANGE JUICE
PEANUTS	STEWARDESS WITH LONG HAIR

ROAD SIGNS

You can photocopy our list or make your own. Color in the signs and laminate if you'd like. Your child can mark the particular sign each time he sees it (you can even write a number over each and have a contest as to who sees the most of each sign).

⭐ *Using local souvenir coloring books is a good way for children to relate to a location they are visiting.*

Be sure to take some finger games with you for those times you and your children have to wait in line.

VACATION

All players begin at the same time. Find the objects in the boxes of the chart one at a time. When someone finds one of the objects, he calls out that he sees it and puts an X on the matching box. An object can be used only by the player who calls it out first. The first player to find eight things across, down, or diagonally in a row wins.

You can customize your card. If you are driving in the summer, replace "snow" with "surfer" or "lifeguard." If you're in the mountains or in Wyoming, replace "swimming pool" with "buffalo." If you are traveling through a city, replace "country" objects with "skyscrapers," "taxis," and "grocery stores."

Sample:

V	A	C	A	T	I	O	N
STOP SIGN	BUS	BLUE CAR	FENCE	CHURCH	ROAD WORKER	NORTH OR SOUTH SIGN	FARM
BIKE	SCHOOL	VAN	SMOKE-STACK	AMUSEMENT PARK	TIRE	HORSE TRAILER	TRAIN TRACK
TRUCK	FRUIT STAND	EAGLE	GAS STATION	COW	MOTEL	SNOW	STATION WAGON
HITCH-HIKER	FLAT TIRE	TRAFFIC LIGHT	POLICE CAR	55 MPH SIGN	MOTOR-CYCLE	SWIMMING POOL	GOLDEN ARCHES
TRAIN	LAKE	DOG	SPRINKLER ON	RIVER BRIDGE	TRACTOR	BOAT	MAN W/ HELMET
HORSE	HOTEL	CONVERTIBLE	FIRE ENGINE	JEEP	TENT	WATER	HOSPITAL
35 MPH SIGN	PICNICKERS	RED FLOWERS	HELICOPTER	BIRD	RED CAR	WATER TOWER	POLICE MOTOR-CYCLE

Road Map Games

ARE WE THERE YET?

On your laminated road map, mark the road you are traveling with one of your markers. Pick a town up ahead that you will come to. Now each player guesses the exact time he thinks the car will arrive at that town. The one who comes closest to guessing the exact time wins the game.

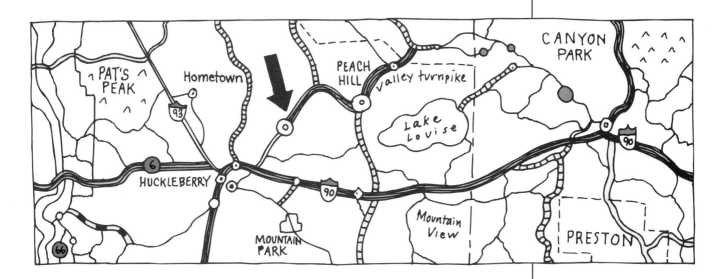

MAP MADNESS

Select two points on your laminated map. Take a marker and trace the red roads that connect them, without lifting the marker from the map. Ask older kids to find: the longest (or shortest) route; a route that doesn't cross water; the route that only uses small roadways (which may mean explaining the color scheme of your map); the route that passes through the most towns. Try using your hometown as the starting point, and then use a city where friends or relatives live as the second point. You can also include cities you have visited or passed through during family vacations.

★ Another tip from Sydny Miner: Don't carry a purse or use the diaper bag — get a waist purse/fanny pack instead. Keep the pouch to the front — it leaves your hands free and you don't need to worry about pickpockets. Also use a backpack so your hands are free to hold your kids' hands.

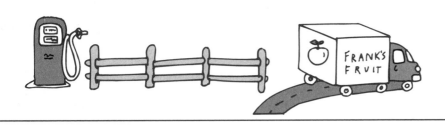

MAP SHAPES

On your laminated map, outline each state with a red marker. Have the kids describe what the shapes of the states remind them of. You can do the same thing on a world map.

★ When the Boorstin kids travel abroad, their parents let them calculate the value of currency on their own calculators. They also chart their trips on the "metro" and "tube" (subways) on miniature maps.

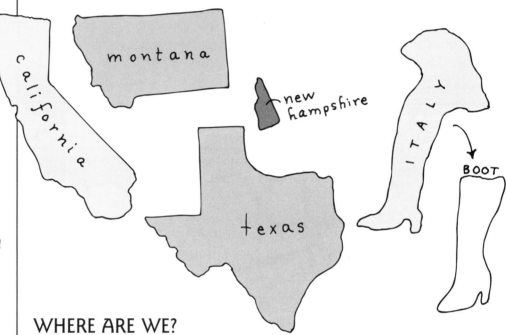

★ Sometimes you may find, to your surprise, that children are less intimidated to try out new things when they are away from home. This was certainly true for Diane and Neil Simon's 9-year-old daughter, Bryn Lander Simon. Bryn always feels stronger about trying out new things when she doesn't have to worry about failing in front of her friends. For example, she learned to swim on a trip to see her grandma in Milwaukee.

WHERE ARE WE?

For this game, you need your laminated map, markers, and a timer. Pick a 5-inch-square portion of your map and mark with a black marker. This is your new "country." Give it a new name (i.e., Juliedom or Fredland).

Your opponent takes the map of your new country and finds a secret city, body of water, or any other location. (Try not to pick the biggest city. Stick to more unusual choices.) Next, your opponent tells you the name of the place he has chosen and you have sixty seconds to find it. If you succeed before time runs out, the number of seconds you took is written down. If you do not find the secret location, your score is 60 and it is your opponent's turn. Play continues with each player taking a turn per round. The player with the lowest point total is the winner.

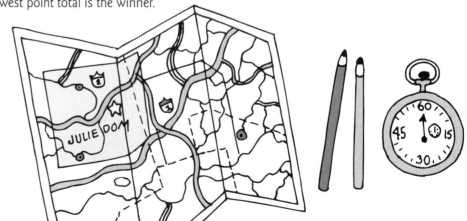

ALL-STATE ROUNDUP

To play this game, you will need one laminated map of the United States and one marker per player. Players look for license plates from the fifty states and record the state name by marking off that state on their map. For a variation, you can also note the colors and state motto from each license plate on a separate piece of paper or on the back of the map. The player with the most state license plates marked off on his map by the end of the day or by the end of the trip wins. If you're playing without a map, just keep a list of the states whose plates you've seen.

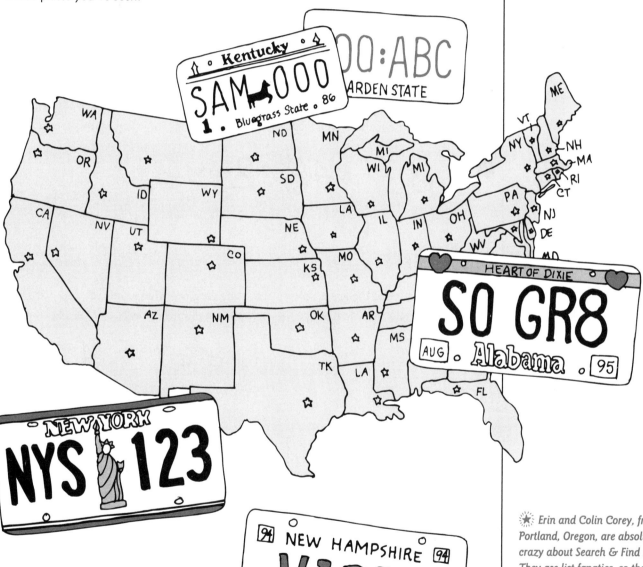

⭐ Erin and Colin Corey, from Portland, Oregon, are absolutely crazy about Search & Find books. They are list fanatics, so these books, available at many airports, make the time go by quickly while the kids are having a ball. And at 99 cents each, you can get more than one for each child.

License Plate Games

MATH WHIZ

When Sonia Israel was 7, her favorite pastime was to multiply numbers because she had just learned the multiplication tables. Every time a car passed, Sonia multiplied the numbers on the license plate as fast as she could. She was so skilled at this that she was sure she invented it (only to find out that people have been playing Math Whiz for years). Play this game alone and see how fast you can tabulate the answer, or call out the numbers and race to see who can come up with the correct answer first. Depending on the ages of the children, an adult may act as a referee, checking to see that the answers are correct.

In another version of Math Whiz, divide the passengers into two teams. As your car passes other cars, look at their license plates and add up the numbers. One team will get a point if the numbers add up to more than 10. The other team will get a point if the numbers add up to less than 10. The team with the most number of points is the winner.

$$8 \times 6 = 48 \times 2 = 96$$

ALPHA-BETS

Using letters found in the license plates of passing cars, see what words you can make that include those letters. If you play against an opponent, keep a list and score one point for each word.

APPLES   APES

LAPS

PAL   SLAP   SALE

PEAS

A, B, C

For young kids, searching for letters of the alphabet is very compelling. Have them call out, in order, each time they find a letter in a road sign or on a passing license plate. You end up looking for an **A**, then a **B**, continuing through **Z**. You *must* find them in order — a MERGE sign may count when you're looking for the **E** but you have to wait to count the **M** until you've found the **L** in another sign. You may find that even older children will enjoy this.

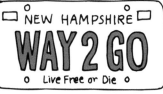

LICENSE PLATE BINGOS

On your laminated bingo card *(see page 58)*, write a different number in each square. As you see the numbers on license plates that match those you've placed in the squares, cross them off your bingo sheet. The first person to cross all the numbers off is the winner. You may adjust the rules to make the game easier or more difficult. For instance, for a challenging version, players may use only one number per plate and that number counts only once. (If you see a 4 on a license plate, you may only cross off one 4 on your card, *and* you may not use any other numbers from that plate.) Or, for an easier game, use as many numbers as you can find on each plate — if you see a plate with a 3, 7, 9, and 2, you may cross off all those numbers on your card. If your card has three 3s, you may cross off all the 3s.

Another version of license plate bingo uses letters. On your card, write a different letter in each square (you can also use graph paper instead of a bingo card). The point of the game is to mark off letters by noting the first letter of passing license plates.

☆ On Gary Gilbar's last flight from L.A. to New York, he sat behind a young child of about 4 or 5. When the movie was about to begin, Gary offered the boy an extra pillow, figuring that he would need it to sit on so he could see the movie above those high seats in front of him. The boy quietly took the pillow and thanked Gary. A few minutes later, Gary looked over and saw — not the child sitting higher, but a periscope peering above the seats! Now, that child will go far!

Guessing and Spotting Games

TIME TRAVEL

The Gilbars have been playing this game for years on their regular trips to Santa Barbara to see the rest of the Gilbar family, and they are still surprised how many variations can be played with this basic game. Guess the amount of time it will take until you see the next billboard, bridge, highway, cow, or whatever you can think of. You can try to guess the distance between towns, road signs, landmarks, bridges, lampposts, or whatever else strikes your fancy.

☀ *Use your timer not only for games but to mark "quiet time" when no one talks.*

CITY SIGNS

When Annie was 12, she loved maps but got tired of reading names she knew nothing about. Her dad then started to name different cities in Pennsylvania and asked everyone to guess what the city is known for. So when Lancaster came up, everyone said, "The Amish." When he said Philadelphia, the answer was "The Liberty Bell." Pittsburgh was quickly identified as a sports center (home of the Pirates and Steelers), while Bethlehem stumped everyone until they arrived there and saw the steel mills.

When the Ancoli clan went to Europe, a new version of the game taught everyone a lot about geography. This time, one player chose a city and kept the name to himself. Each passenger asked a question about that mystery city (for example, "Is the city on the Seine River?," "Does it have a famous art museum?," or "Is it famous for hot dogs?"). When someone guessed the answer, a new city was picked and the game began again.

THE BROKAW MILE

The driver notes the mileage on the gauge and says "Go." Each of the passengers takes a turn in guessing when a mile has passed. In the Brokaw family, Andrea guessed accurately time and again. It's good to have another game in mind so that the driver can shut this one down when he doesn't want to look at the odometer one more time.

CAR CARDS

Make sixteen small cards (about 3 inches by 5 inches). On each one, write a category, such as states, countries, vacation spots, state flowers, artists, books, sports figures, politicians, presidents, movies, celebrities, rock groups, or songs. (You can also use cards from your favorite memory game.)

Place the pack face down. The first player calls out a letter of the alphabet, turns up the top card, and reads the category aloud. The first player to name something in that category, beginning with the letter called, gets that card. That player then calls a letter of the alpha-bet and picks a card from the pile. The game continues until all sixteen cards have been chosen. The winner is the player with the most cards in his hand.

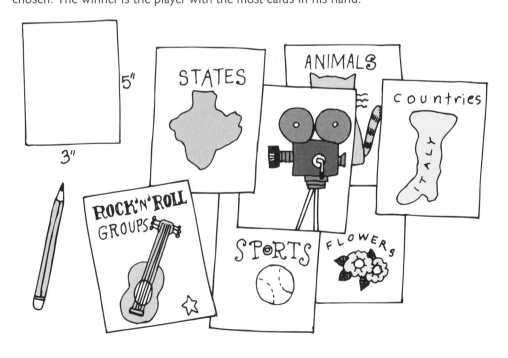

GOT IT!

This was a favorite of the Brokaw girls on their many car trips around the country. Just remember — the driver can't play!

Everyone looks out the window and picks something far away — a building, a bridge, a billboard — and then everyone but the driver shuts his eyes. Whenever someone thinks the chosen sight is near, he yells out, "Got it!" The player whose guess is the closest wins.

WHO AM I?

This game is a perennial favorite because it is a child's chance to be a famous person. Someone pretends he is a celebrity but doesn't say whom he has chosen. Everyone else tries to guess who he is by asking questions, one at a time, which can be answered only with a "yes" or "no." Whoever guesses the correct person gets a chance to be the next star.

Here's another version of Who Am I? In this one, the leader also thinks of a famous person and tells the others the first letter of his last name. But the difference is this: If you choose to be George Washington and give the letter W, the first player asks a *general* question — "Are you an author?" — and the leader answers by saying, "No, I am not Edith Wharton." "Are you an actor or actress?" is the next question. "No, I am not Bruce Willis." Play continues until someone guesses the celebrity answer. If you can't come up with a "W" name for a category, the person who asked the question must answer it.

For younger kids, you can limit the game by having them choose to be a cartoon character or a character in a book that they have read.

★ *A direct route to kids' hearts is through their stomachs, says Sharon Boorstin. "When going to a new place, we always make a big deal of introducing the kids to local cuisine, whether it is fresh shrimp and hush puppies in Hilton Head Island, South Carolina, gingerbread cookies in Colonial Williamsburg, pretzels on the street in New York, or baguette sandwiches on the Left Bank in Paris. "This past June in Paris, 9-year-old Adam tried escargot (he liked them), and both he and his sister, Julia, became connoisseurs of French and Italian ice creams."*

ON SALE

Here is a novel way to buy and sell without using money. The game has lots of kid appeal, and the things they come up with will entertain parents for miles.

One player owns a store of his choosing and all players have to guess what he is selling there. Whoever guesses the correct answer gets to open his own store. For example, one child starts by saying, "I own a camping store and I sell something that starts with the letter T." Each of the other players gets three chances to guess what he is selling. If a player guesses correctly (tents, for example) and he is right, he gets to "open" his own store. If a player guesses incorrectly, the owner of the store tells him what he is selling and he gets to sell again with a new letter.

★ *Lisa Gilbar's favorite game is Cow-Bury. The object of this game is to see who can find the most cows when traveling by car or train. Each player takes one side of the road and counts the number of cows he sees. But when you pass a cemetery on your side, you must bury all the cows you've counted up to that point and start over. Set a time limit.*

SPELLBACK

This game is primarily for children who are able to spell, but it can also be played by pre-readers. The degree of difficulty is controlled by which word you choose. Have a child select a word and write it backward on a piece of paper. The other players take turns guessing the word. The fun part comes when you all try to sound out the backward word. If you like, use your timer — the ticking sound only heightens the excitement.

SPOT SPOT

From the very beginning of the trip until you return home, keep one list of every animal you see (if a zoo is on your itinerary, make sure you have extra paper). You will be astonished at the number of different animals you will encounter on your trip, even in a city. It's a lot of fun, your kids will learn a lot, and you'll find that the task itself will keep them from getting bored no matter where they are.

SIGNALS

Here's a new use for the car radio.

One player sits in the front seat and watches the station numbers in the display window as he presses the **SCAN** or **SEEK** button on the radio. The first player tells the second player the "signal" that comes up in the display window. The second player then begins a one-minute search outside the car on license plates, road signs, building numbers, and billboards for the numbers that make up the "signal." Players receive a point each time they spot one of the numbers in the station number called. The winner is the player with the most points at the end of three rounds.

 *When reading an article, singing a tune, or telling a story, omit an important word and see if your child can guess what it is. Younger children will enjoy this game if played using familiar passages from their favorite stories or songs.*

PASS BY

Keep a pad of paper and a pen handy. As you pass other cars, billboards, signs, stores, or other sights, have each child call out something funny she sees and you keep the list. Personalized license plates, funny sayings around the rims of license plates or on bumper stickers, signs in restaurant windows all count. You'll get a kick out of reading these at the end of each day. When you return home, the long list will help you remember those fun times when you collected the names. It's also an unusual addition to your trip memory book.

WHAT'S THAT?

Look out the window, pick an object, and describe its size, its shape, what it does, and who might use it. After each description the child gets three chances to guess what you've just described. Continue until your child guesses correctly, and then switch places.

Favorite Old-Time Car Games

Annie and her sister, Sonia, took many car trips with their parents all over the country. They both remember never tiring of games that were simply about the cars around them. As the tradition continues with their children, here are five of their all-time favorite games.

MY FRIEND POLICEMAN

Whenever you see a policeman (in a squad car, in a highway patrol car, or on a motorcycle), you yell out, "My Friend Policeman." Whoever spots the policeman first gets the credit. You can continue this game for hours. Even while playing other games, you can keep score on spotting the policeman (or woman).

COLOR CARS

Each person chooses a color. Then each player counts how many cars of his color he finds in a certain period of time.

CAR LOT

Car Lot is another favorite car game. The object is to spot and count different kinds of cars — trucks, buses, convertibles, vans, motorcycles, four-wheel-drive vehicles, or others. You can keep a tally playing alone or against an opponent.

If you have room in your car, carry some individual tissue boxes, as public restrooms are often out of toilet paper.

NEXT!

In this game, everyone must look straight ahead. Each player must guess the color of the next car that will pass you. You get one point for each correct guess. To add to the challenge, if you correctly guess a *kind* of car (bus, van, convertible, semi truck) you get an extra 3 points.

☀ *During the Bilskys' trip to the Pacific Northwest, they began every dinner with Lee drawing pictures of the new places they had seen that day — the Golden Gate Bridge, the Bay Bridge, cable cars, the zoo, etc. It was entertaining for him, and it helped pass the time waiting for dinner.*

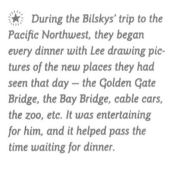

GOTCHA!

Annie's favorite niece, Sarah Israel, is a fanatic about driving safely. Not only can she spot a car changing lanes without signaling before anyone else can, she's also a champ at using her X-ray eyes to see who's not wearing a seat belt — in a passing car!

Try this with your kids in the car. It's a fun game for children (they love to catch adults doing something wrong) and it's also educational. You'll be surprised how safety-conscious your children will become after playing!

To play, call out any obvious traffic violation you see. Keep score to see who can spot the most. Obvious ones to watch out for include speeding, not stopping at a stop sign, littering, driving in a car pool lane without any passengers, having no brake lights, or cutting off another driver.

BRIGHT NIGHT

This is a great game to play at night, especially when everyone is tired and you can't wait to reach your destination. The object is to find things that are lit and keep score. The one who calls out the most wins. Look for street lamps, traffic lights, cars with only one light (headlights or brake lights), neon signs, store signs, lights on inside a moving vehicle, stars, the moon. You can spot and call out more than one of each. For example, each time you see another lit motel sign, it counts as another score.

COPY CAT

In Copy Cat, players win points for getting people in other cars to copy what they are doing. Try playing while stopped at a gas station, in a restaurant, or at a red light. Players can clap their hands, cover their eyes, wiggle their noses, pull on their ears, fold their arms, rub their eyes, or wave.

FLIPBOOK BEGINS HERE!

Layovers are not much fun — the kids are tired and restless, and the planes are always late taking off. The people at the Denver air-port figured out a solution. Look for the kids' area with toys, science exhibits, a room full of balls to play in, and a full-time guard.

Puzzles

MAP PUZZLES

Glue the map of your upcoming vacation spot to a piece of foamboard. For young children, cut the map into a few larger pieces. For older children, cut the map into a number of smaller pieces. Store in an envelope.

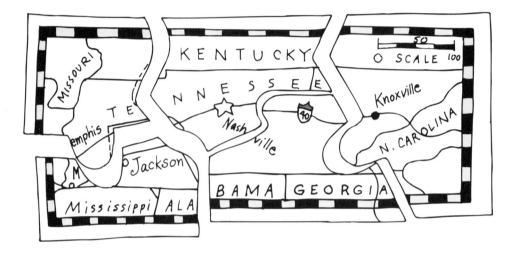

MINI PUZZLES

Mini Puzzles can be purchased at toy stores, but you can make your own by cutting up a postcard, a Christmas card, or a small map. Store your little puzzles in a plastic travel soap container.

★ *Audio tapes of music and read-aloud stories are a good way to pass the time for kids too young to play games or read to themselves. Dorian Hastings makes her own read-aloud tapes of her son's books so he can read his books and hear her voice at the same time.*

Chatter Games

TALL TALES

This game is fun to play in the car, or while waiting in line for a table in a restaurant. One player begins telling a "tall tale" and stops at an exciting point. The next player continues the story and stops for another player to construct the action. Set a time limit for your story or just see where the plot leads.

PIG LATIN

Learning a foreign language by listening to tapes can be fun, but another tongue that children can learn in minutes is Pig Latin. Take off the first letter or phonetic sound of a word and add it after the last letter, then add an "ay." If the word begins with a vowel, add "vay." "Shall we play a game?" would become "Allshay eway ayplay avay amegay?" It's better, of course, if they think no one else has the code.

A B CITIES

The first player names a city. In turn, each player names another city that starts with the same letter of the alphabet as the first city named. For instance, if the first player says "New York," the next player can say "Nantucket," and the third "Naples." If a player can't name one, he's out and the last player wins and chooses another city to play again.

THE PRINCIPAL'S PUPPY

Each player gets to name a characteristic of the Principal's Puppy. The object is to see how silly your descriptions can be. The first player begins: "The principal's puppy is a perky puppy." The next player has to describe the principal's puppy using any other words that begin with **P**. He may say "pesky," "pretty," "private," or "plush." When all the players run out of adjectives beginning with **P**, they choose another letter and start again.

The new mini-toys for kids, like Polly Pocket or Mighty Max, are perfect for small-space play and come in their own "environments."

MOM'S COOKIE JAR

Grandma Sylvia Gilbar swears this game kept her twins, Gary and Steven, busy forever! Here's how to play: The first player says, "In my mom's cookie jar, I found a cookie." The next player says, "In my mom's cookie jar, I found a cookie and a hat." The third player adds an object and play continues until the sequence is too long to remember.

ONE, TWO, THREE

The object of One, Two, Three is to name as many words as you can to rhyme with numbers. For example, start with one: "fun, run, bun." Continue with two: "blue, you, zoo." Then three: "free, tree, me." Think of as many words to rhyme with each number as you can and then move on to the next number. See how high you can go.

Jonathan and Jennie Tucker pass the time while traveling in other countries by playing simple "money" and "time" games with respective currency ("How many yen to the dollar" or "If it's 3 A.M. in Japan, what time is it at home in Boston?").

MATCH IT

To play Match It, the players choose a category, such as the circus. Each player must name something associated with the circus. Play continues until someone repeats something or can't think of a match. Pick a new category and start again.

WHAT IF . . . ?

Young children love this game and are particularly good at it since their imaginations are not limited by reality. Name an unusual situation that is not possible but whose consequences would be dramatic and funny. For example, ask your child, "What if adults had to go to school and kids got to stay home or go to work?" or "What if dogs could talk?" The results will be remarkable enough for you to note down the answers.

NEWS REPORTER

Give your child a microphone to hold (it doesn't have to be a real one — he can turn a powder brush or a flashlight into a "pretend" microphone). Ask him to report on what he sees out of the window. Encourage him to be precise yet imaginative, and to include not only stationary things he sees but experiences as well. ("There's a bus passing by and the driver waves his hat as he honks his horn to pass us on the left.") You can each take turns playing reporter and award an "Emmy" for best broadcast.

THE AD AGE

Pretend you are in the advertising business. Our friend Cliff Einstein has come up with sayings for many well-known products. When his boys were little, they would play a game in which each of them would try to come up with his own slogan for his favorite things. Make a list of your child's favorite foods, sports accessories, movies, books, and toys and have everyone try his or her hand at coming up with advertising slogans.

★ *Before Joshua Gordon was a teen-ager, his favorite traveling pastime was collecting recipes from different countries. When he returned home, he would make those dishes for the whole family.*

RADIO DAYS

Announce that you have found a station with a program called "The Mystery Hour." Each person then takes turns being the announcer and weaving a story of intrigue. Keep taking turns until the storytellers reach a conclusion. When done, pretend to be broadcast reporters for a talk show with a funny topic ("Today we'll talk to women named Sally who let their kids cook their own dinner — what will they make?"), a baseball game, a cooking show, or a call-in show. The endless possibilities will result in entertaining commentary for all.

TONGUE TWISTERS

Try our list of twisters or make up your own:

> The two-toed tiger tried to tiptoe, too.
>
> Molly made many monkeys mind Mom.
>
> Silly Sally sold stockings Sunday.
>
> Fourteen frail friends found firecrackers frightening.
>
> While Willy's worms whined, Warren's wasted waffles waited.
>
> Ellie's elegant elephant eagerly entered the elevator.
>
> Any annoying angel angered Annie's aunt annually.
>
> Has Hallie's happy holiday happened?
>
> Rubber baby-buggy bumper

⭐ HELLO

Try these different ways to say hello. This works great when your trip has many stops and your child can try out his new vocabulary on waiters, hotel clerks, and gas station attendants.

FRENCH: Bonjour

DUTCH: Goeden dag

GERMAN: Guten tag

ITALIAN: Buon giorno

HEBREW: Shalom

JAPANESE: Konichee-wa

SPANISH: Buenos días

NO, NO

Everyone decides on one word that cannot be spoken, such as "their, there, and they're" or "mom" or "I or eye." Then start a conversation while trying to trick one another into saying the "No, No" word. When someone says the forbidden word, he gets a "P.P." (penalty point). At the end of ten miles, count up the P.P.s; the one with the least, wins.

WEIRD WILLY

Weird Willy has strange tastes. Each player takes a turn being Weird Willy. The first Weird Willy might say, "I love sandwiches but I hate ice cream." Weird Willy has not given the other players a clue as to why, so Weird Willy continues. "I love sour cream but I hate doughnuts." Still no clue? "I love soda but I hate candy." Someone might guess that Weird Willy loves anything that starts with the letter **S**. The person who guesses correctly gets to be the next Weird Willy. He might say, "I love tea but I hate television." No clue? Then, "I love the top but I hate the bottom." Pretty soon someone guesses that Willy likes things that begin with **T** and have three letters.

Lisa Gilbar's last great win on a trip to Santa Barbara went like this: "I love squirrels but I hate monkeys." Not even one guess. "I love Mommy but I hate Mom." What? "I love school and all my classes but I hate learning." Finally Lisa's dad got it: "Lisa loves anything with a double letter in its spelling!"

This game made a two-hour trip go by in a flash!

MAMA MIA!

This can be played by kids of nearly all ages. The main player selects an action verb like "hop," "cry," or "giggle." To find the secret word, other players ask questions substituting the phrase "Mama Mia!" for the word they're looking for. The main player must answer every question by using the phrase "Mama Mia!" instead of the secret action verb.

When Marc Gilbar was 8, his favorite words were "itch," "tickle," and "scream." So Marc would keep the word "itch" in his head and Annie would ask, "Would I 'Mama Mia!'?" And he would answer, "Yes, you would 'Mama Mia!'" Lisa might then say, "Would a cat 'Mama Mia!'?" Marc would answer, "Yes, a cat would 'Mama Mia!'" Eventually someone will figure out the secret action verb. You might want to limit the number of times each player may guess.

Jenny MacKenzie gives her children travel-size Etch-A-Sketch to entertain them without pencil and paper.

Pencil-and-Paper Games

These are a set of our all-time-favorite pencil-and-paper games from *The Penny Whistle Sick-in-Bed Book*.

SHIPS AT SEA

This game works best with two players. You will need a pad of ¼-inch graph paper, two pencils, and two 6-inch rulers. First you must make your game sheets (see drawing). For each board, draw a box measuring 10 squares by 10 squares at the top of the page. Repeat at the bottom of the page. Write the numbers 1 through 10 above each square in the top line. Write the letters **A** through **J** beside each square in the first vertical line. Repeat in the box below. Label the top box "Mine"; the bottom box, "The Enemy."

To play, each person takes a game board and in the box marked "Mine" hides the four different kinds of ships in straight lines − up and down or across − in random spots. (See drawing: The battleship occupies 5 squares, the cruiser is 4, the destroyer is 3, and the submarine is 2.) Label your ships. Don't allow your opponent to see your sheet. He will be attempting to guess where you've hidden your ships, while you are trying to find his ships. The players take turns calling out coordinates. If your opponent calls **F7**, you put an X in square **F7** in the "Mine" box. If your opponent hits one of your ships, you must tell your opponent he has a hit and he will put an X in square **F7** in his "Enemy" box.

Now it is your turn. You may say **A2**. If your opponent tells you that you have a hit, put an X in square **A2** in your "Enemy" box; he will put an X in **A2** in his "Mine" box. As all the ships have been placed horizontally and vertically, you will know that you should hit up and down, to the right or left of a square, until you "sink" one of his ships. A player wins when he has destroyed all of his opponent's ships.

BATTLESHIP
5 BOXES

CRUISER
4 BOXES

DESTROYER
3 BOXES

SUBMARINE
2 BOXES

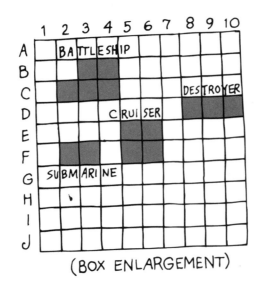

(BOX ENLARGEMENT)

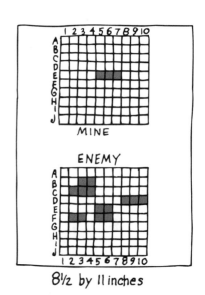

MINE

ENEMY

8½ by 11 inches

THE WORDSMITH GAME

Here's a game that will give your child's vocabulary a workout. It is a little like Scrabble, and can be played with as many people as you like or with just two. Each player has a game sheet on which you have drawn a box 5 squares by 5 squares. (If your child can write very small legible letters, try using graph paper, marking off a large box so there will be a finite number of squares for the letters.) The first player calls out any letter of the alphabet. Each player writes in the letter anywhere he wants to on his game sheet. Then the next player calls out a letter, and the players put it down anywhere. The object is to build as many words as possible from the letters, going up and down or across but not on the diagonal. The game continues, each player calling out a letter, until all the squares are filled. The player using the most letters to form words is the winner. (For kids over 12, you can make the game more challenging by making more or fewer squares, or by permitting words on the diagonal as well as up, down, and across.)

   A variation of this is "Foursomes." Each player gets a game sheet on which you have drawn a box 4 squares by 4 squares. The first player calls out any letter he likes. All the players write it down in any one of the 16 squares. The second player calls out a letter, and so on, until 16 letters have been called. The object of the game is to put the letters in the squares in such a way that they form four-letter words. The player with the most words wins. Words may be formed across, diagonally, up, or down.

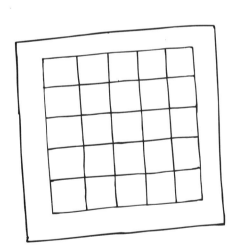

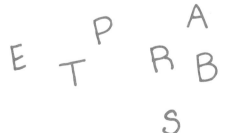

☀ *A bed tray with legs is perfect for a child to use as a work space while seated in the car.*

CONNECTIONS

To play, take a piece of graph paper, using one sheet for each game, no matter how many players are involved. Draw dots to form squares (see drawing). Each player takes a turn drawing a line between the dots. When a player completes a square, he writes his initial in it so he knows it's his. A player who completes a square gets to go again. (This means that he can sometimes complete several squares, one after another.) When all the dots are connected, the person with the most squares wins.

For a variation, you can make this "Five in a Row." The object is for each player to get five of his boxes in a row, up and down, across, or diagonally. Each player in turn tries to block the others from getting five in a row.

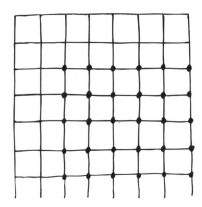

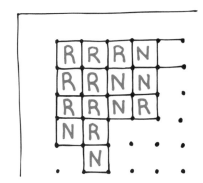

"Remember — don't take your child's favorite toy if it has too many pieces," suggests Jan Levine. "You always lose some in an airplane, and even if you can crawl around and actually find the missing piece, you'll make all the other passengers around you crazy!" Actually, Cara Levine once lost a favorite doll on an airplane, so the Levines try to take new things rather than risk losing old favorites. "But," Jan reminds, "make sure you try out all new toys before you pack them. There's nothing worse than sitting on an airplane and starting to play with a new toy only to find there is a piece missing or it breaks on the first try!"

SQUIGGLES AND WIGGLES

Begin by drawing a short wiggly line on a piece of paper. Your child must study the line and make some kind of drawing out of it. You will find that you can make figures, animals, houses, or anything else by turning the paper sideways, upside down, or any other way. If more than two people play, each makes a wiggly line on his paper and then gives it to the player next to him for that player to use as his starting point.

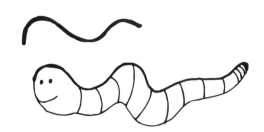

TWIN NUMBER MAZE

All you need for this game is a pencil and paper. On a large sheet of paper write the numbers 1 through 20 so that they are randomly scattered. Now write the numbers 1 through 20 again all over the paper, trying not to have matching numbers near each other. (To make an alphabet maze, use the letters **A** through **Z** in place of numbers.)

   The object of the game is to connect the duplicate numbers (or letters) with pencil lines without touching or crossing another line. Each player in turn connects two matching numbers with a line, starting with the single digits and proceeding in order through the 20s.
 You don't have to draw the shortest route between two numbers. If you want to mess up the other player's track, just draw a long, winding line. Usually the game begins to get tough when you reach the midteens. The first player who can't connect two matching numbers without his line touching or crossing another line loses.

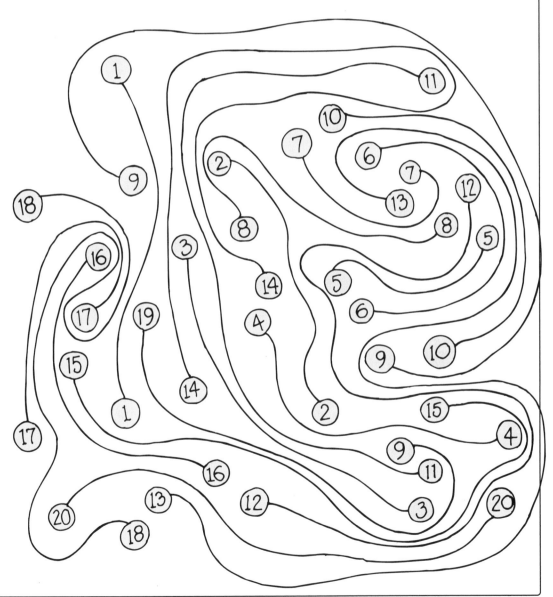

HINT ☆
CIRCLE THE
NUMBERS AS
YOU CONNECT
THEM.

☀ These pencil-and-paper
games are great to play on paper
place mats to keep everyone busy
at restaurants.

DON'T CROSS ME

The first player draws a house with a chimney and surrounds it with twelve to twenty dots. The second player shows him what dot to circle. The first player starts from the chimney and draws a line circling the dot. The second player carries the line from the circled dot to the next one indicated by the first player, and so on, until all the dots are circled. The player with the last turn then must take the line back to the chimney. All this must be done without touching or crossing any lines.

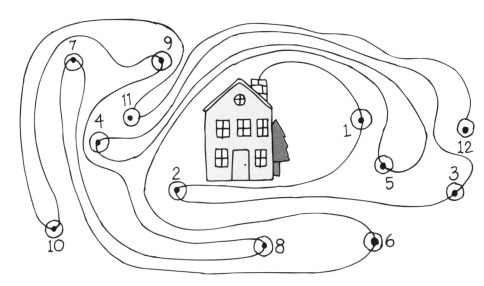

HINT ☆ BE SURE TO LEAVE ENOUGH ROOM AROUND THE HOUSE. [x]

THE SNAKE

To begin, mark ten rows of ten dots each on a sheet of paper. The first player draws a horizontal or vertical line to join any two adjacent dots; diagonal lines are not allowed. The second player then draws another line, connecting either end of the existing line horizontally or vertically to any adjacent dot. The players then continue playing alternately in this manner, drawing a line from either end of the existing line ("the snake") to an adjacent dot. The object is to force your opponent into a position in which he has to draw a line that will connect either end of the snake back to itself, thus causing him to lose the game.

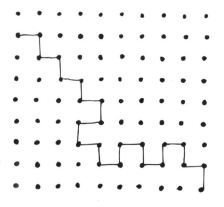

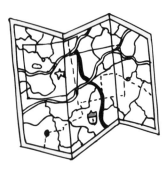

★ When Steve and Ronna Feldman traveled from New York to Washington by car, their parents, Lillian and Murray, gave them maps and let them mark the spots where they wanted to stop. The kids took turns choosing one stop every 100 miles. They had to add and subtract the number of miles noted on the roads and then figure out where they wanted to plan their stops.

TAXI!

On a sheet of paper, write the numbers 1 through 21 in random order in three parallel lines across the page, each line of numbers representing a street and each number a house. In the upper left-hand corner, draw a little square for the garage of the taxi driver. One player is the taxi driver and the other is the passenger. The passenger directs the driver to take him to a house – say, number 11 on First Street. The driver must draw a line from the garage to house number 11. The passenger may then say, "Drive me to 6 Third Street," and the driver draws a line from number 11 to number 6, but must not cross the previous line. The passenger may call any house number that he chooses, but may go to each house only once.

This goes on until the driver can't go to the address asked for without crossing one of his previous lines. His turn as taxi driver then ends, and he counts the number of houses that he has visited; that is his score.

The players then change roles for a new diagram; the one who was the driver becomes the passenger and vice versa. The driver who has visited the most houses is the winner. Your child can also play alone by calling out his own numbers.

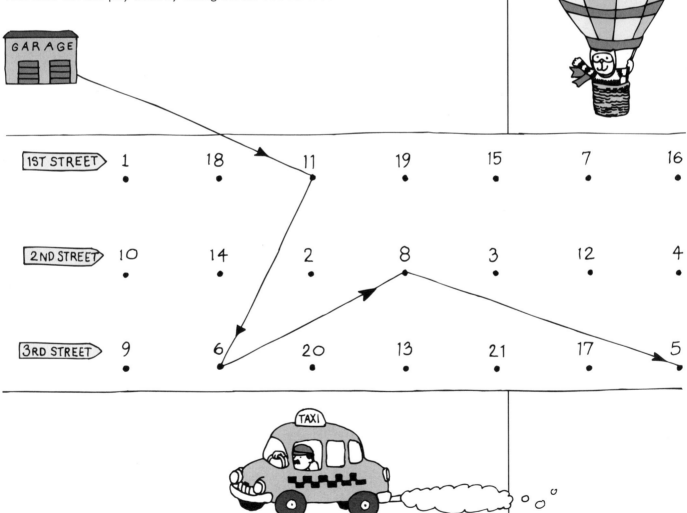

☆ *Try coloring all the vehicles without once using the same color twice.*

The Penny Whistle Road Adventure

"The Penny Whistle Road Adventure" *(see pages 90-91)* is five fun-filled action-packed games rolled into one. We suggest that before you hit the road you make plenty of photo-copies of "The Penny Whistle Road Adventure" so that all your travelers will be well pre-pared to play their favorites over and over again.

ROAD WAY

Younger children will enjoy playing "Road Way" in which the only rule is to let your imagi-nation run wild. Using a copy of "The Penny Whistle Road Adventure," colored pencils and crayons, a player colors the scene the way he wishes. After players have finished color-ing in our drawing, have them try to draw their own cars, roads signs, or anything they can think of on the Road Adventure.

CAR LOT

"Car Lot" is an easy game for any age. Using crayons or colored pencils and lots of creativi-ty, color in all the vehicles you can find on "The Penny Whistle Road Adventure." Or you might want to choose one color for all the cars found, another color for all the trucks found, and yet another color for all the buses.

TRAFFIC JAM

"Traffic Jam" is a variation on "Car Lot." After you've colored in all the cars, buses, and trucks you can find, count the number of different kinds of vehicles you've colored. Older children might enjoy playing this part of the game while being timed. How long does it take you to color all the cars? If there are two or more players, take turns coloring and see which player can count the most cars in a given time period or who can count all the cars in the least amount of time.

BILLBOARD BINGO

This game uses a copy of "The Penny Whistle Road Adventure" as a bingo board. One or many can play this game by simply recording their favorite road signs or billboards as they see them. The first to finish can be the winner, or maybe the player with 20 of the funniest signs should win!

GET READY, GET SET... WHERE'S PENNY CAT?

Somewhere hiding in the midst of all the traffic, all the signs, all the trees, you will find Penny Cat. Time yourself and see how long it takes you to locate Penny Cat. Or for a variation, have a race between two players. Each player will have his or her own copy of "The Penny Whistle Road Adventure." A third player will be needed to time the two players as they search the landscape for Penny Cat. Whoever is the first to find Penny Cat wins.

★ *As a variation on "Get Ready, Get Set, Where's Penny Cat?," draw a tiny picture of your favorite pet somewhere in the drawing and see how long it takes everyone to find it.*

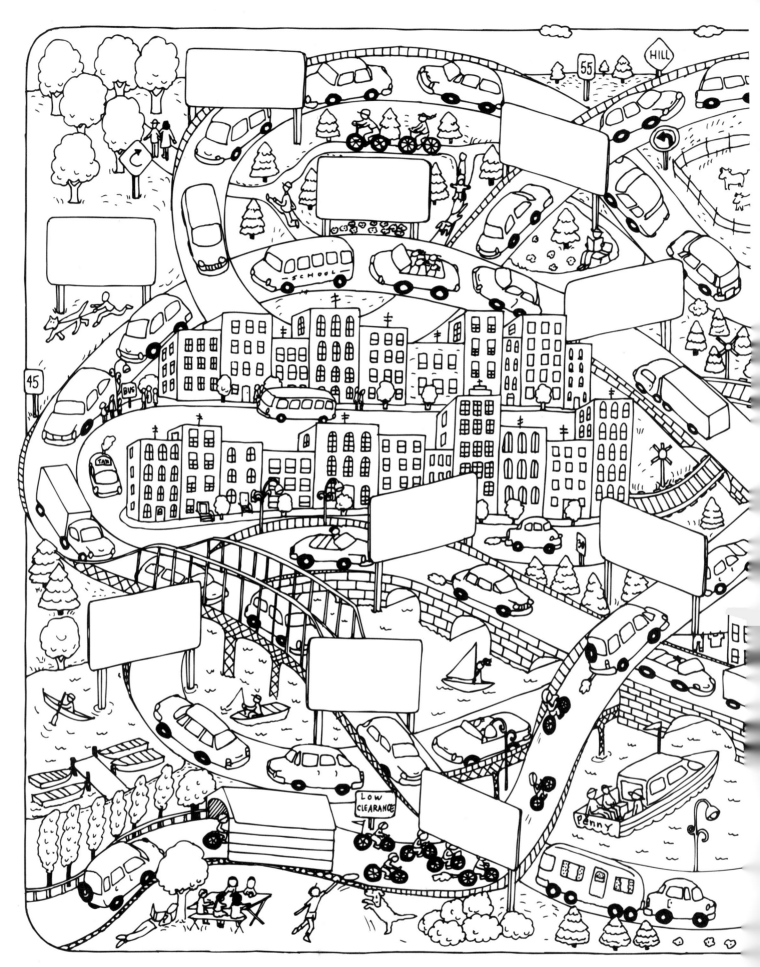

55

HILL

45

BUS

TAXI

SCHOOL

LOW
CLEARANCE

PENNY

90

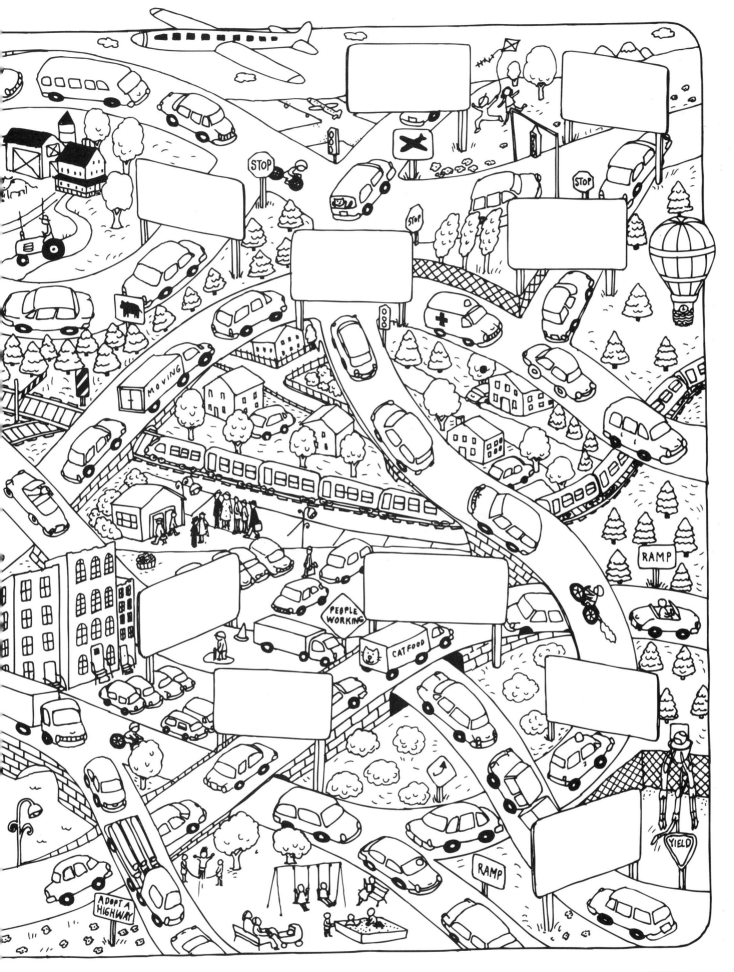

STOP

STOP

STOP

MOVING

RAMP

PEOPLE
WORKING

CAT FOOD

RAMP

YIELD

ADOPT A
HIGHWAY

91

Miniature Magnetic Travel Games

★ Lego sells a foundation for their building blocks that is perfect for use while traveling. Check your local toy store.

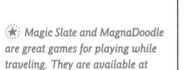

★ Magic Slate and MagnaDoodle are great games for playing while traveling. They are available at most toy stores.

BACKGAMMON (Pressman)

CHECKERS/CHESS (Pressman)

OUTBURST JR. TRAVEL (Western)

PERIL (Pressman)

POCKET SIMON (Milton Bradley)

SESAME STREET TRAVEL (International Games)

TRAVEL BATTLESHIP (Milton Bradley)

TRAVEL BOGGLE (Parker Brothers)

TRAVEL CHINESE CHECKERS (Pressman)

TRAVEL CLUE (Parker Brothers)

TRAVEL CONNECT FOUR (Milton Bradley)

TRAVEL CROCODILE DENTIST (Milton Bradley)

TRAVEL GUESS WHO? (Milton Bradley)

TRAVEL HOT SHOT BASKETBALL (Milton Bradley)

TRAVEL LABYRINTH (Cardinal)

TRAVEL MAGNADOODLE (Tyco)

TRAVEL MASTERMIND (Pressman)

TRAVEL MEMORY (Milton Bradley)

TRAVEL MONOPOLY JUNIOR (Parker Brothers)

TRAVEL PASS THE PIGS (Milton Bradley)

TRAVEL PERFECTION (Milton Bradley)

TRAVEL SCRABBLE (Milton Bradley)

TRAVEL SHARK ATTACK! (Milton Bradley)

TRAVEL SORRY! (Parker Brothers)

TRAVEL TROUBLE (Milton Bradley)

TRAVEL YAHTZEE (Milton Bradley)

★ *Keep a penlight in your glove compartment.*

★ *Lisa Gilbar visits her Aunt Janice in Lyme, New Hampshire, every year. She knows that when she gets home, her Auntie Jan will send her a "Memory Album" with pictures, mementos, stickers, and very silly captions.*

Keeping track of your trip is not only fun while you are doing it, but also preserves the adventure for the future. Once your kids have the task of collecting mementos for their travelogue, they will see things with new enthusiasm and collect them with great vigilance.

There are some tools your family should assemble ahead of time so your record-keeping journey can begin the moment the wheels start to move. There are many different ways of logging a journey, so take note of our possibilities and then decide to either choose one or combine several methods.

The most common travel record is a written journal. This works best for children who are very comfortable writing. (It never works to force a child who finds writing a chore to keep this kind of journal — in fact, getting him to start with a pictorial or video journal may bring him around to try the written record the next trip.) Since your child will need a blank book, you might give him one as a gift (along with a special pencil or pen) specifically for the trip or have him choose his own.

Once you are out on the road, try to make a specific time for everyone to record their memories. Making notes every day at the same time is a good habit to get into, even when some days may produce only one sentence. If it is a one-sentence day, make sure the most outstanding sight or happening is included. That may be all that's needed to jog the memory in years to come.

You can also include your Penny Whistle passport, postcard, and travel certificate in the travelogue *(see pages 44 and 46-49).*

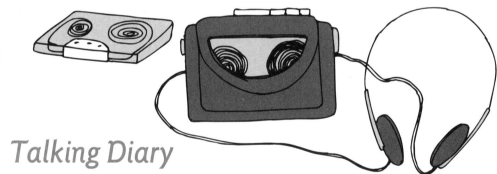

Talking Diary

Audio recorders are an especially good way to keep track of a vacation for children of any age, particularly preschoolers. By articulating on tape all that he's noticing, your child probably will notice and remember more. (Besides, having his young voice on tape will be priceless when he is older.)

You will need an audio recorder plus several blank tapes. Have your child record his thoughts on the road, while sightseeing, in the restaurant, and at the end of the day. He may want to interview his family members, ask questions about what they like most about the trip. He may also enjoy speaking to people he meets during the course of the vacation. The audio diary will vary in detail according to the age of your child.

Sentence Travelogue

This travelogue (perfect for the child who is a reluctant writer) requires just a minute each day but by the end of your trip, you'll have recorded hours of fun. On the first day of your trip write your destination and the date. Every evening before you go to bed, write *one* sentence about what you did or saw during the day. It is sometimes helpful for everyone to reminisce about the day's events, since that helps children focus on the event or observation that stands out in their minds. Remember — this is your child's journal. It is his memory, no matter how silly or trivial it may sound to someone else, that matters.

Younger children who are just beginning to write may need some help. Older kids might find it frustrating to write only one sentence, particularly on those fun-packed days. But the body of work will become more impressive as a whole, and while the first two days of the trip they might complain "one sentence is not enough," more often than not by the seventh or eighth day one sentence will be "just right."

You can also turn the day's events into a story that grows over the course of the trip and add one illustration per day as well.

 Sometimes when the Tuckers take the kids to Europe they have to be taken out of school for short periods of time. Besides doing some of their homework on the trip, the kids also keep complete books of their travels, writing daily entries and including post-cards, stamps, matchbook covers, and photographs. Not only do the kids love looking at these books time after time, but the teachers back home are also fascinated by their collections of memories when they are shared with the classes.

Junior Journal

For younger members of the trip who can write simple words, buy a blank notebook and with markers write "My Trip" on the front cover. On the first page have your child write her name and age, and paste in her favorite photo of herself. In the rest of the journal, let this child write a word or two on each page as she likes, but collect pictures, postcards, stickers, and any other miniature items that she can then paste into this journal. As the trip progresses, you can ask your child to draw the things and people she saw as soon as you get back to the car, when they are fresh in her mind. At the end of the day, your child may want to add more pictures or have you help her glue mementos from the day into her journal.

Nature Walk Diary

This is a perfect diary to keep when you are camping or vacationing in the outdoors and is appropriate for both younger and older children. To keep a Nature Walk Diary you need a notebook, markers, a glue stick, a small stapler, and some envelopes. Collect flowers, leaves, stones, shells, or any small and portable items you find. Press flowers and leaves between the pages of your notebook. Staple small envelopes to the pages and store small stones or shells. Jot down any thoughts you have about your surroundings. Sketch pictures of landscapes, seascapes, trees, and animals you see. Be sure to leave room for adding photographs when you get home.

Photo Journal

Although not everybody enjoys experiencing a trip through a viewfinder, a photographic record can be enjoyed for years to come. All you need is an inexpensive camera and several rolls of black-and-white or color film (or a disposable camera or two, which are now available with wide-angle lenses) for each child. Buy a photo album for each child and have it waiting for him at home. Or, if you are traveling around the country by car and have the time to develop the film at one-hour photo places as you go along, bring the photo album with you. Filling the album with photos every night becomes a wonderful activity. Lisa and Marc Gilbar used two albums each on their trip through New England to celebrate their dad's birthday. Every night at the next motel the kids would fill in their albums with the pictures they had taken the day before, stickers (Dartmouth College, Monmouth Museum) that they collected from various sights, and funny sayings they picked up at the local photo-developing store. Their dad added his special touch when he drew a little cartoon on each page.

★: If you can, take your film to a one-hour photo developer so you can see the pictures while you are still traveling; include them as part of your daily diary.

Story Time

The audio or videotape recorder can be used to record a story or make a movie that is based on either your real or your fantasy vacation. Besides comments on the food and sights, reviews of restaurants and accommodations, include songs you sing, jokes, and funny stories. You can also add sound effects to your production:

GALLOPING HORSE: *Slap your hands on your thighs.*
KNOCK ON THE DOOR: *Click your tongue.*
WIND: *Crumple a piece of paper or whistle.*
RUNNING: *Knock on glass window with knuckles very fast.*
OTHER SOUNDS: *Speak in different voices for different characters.*
　　　　　Beep the horn.
　　　　　Jingle keys.

★: Always take extra batteries in the car so tape recorders are ready for making travelogues.

Bobby and Jonny Miner (6 and 4, respectively) are crazy about Broadway musicals. When they travel by car they play the tapes, with everyone taking a different part to sing along. Their mom, Sydny, has also used this opportunity to play music from shows the kids don't know. She figures having such a captive audience is the best time to introduce them to her favorites.

When Mary Slawson traveled with her children, Laurette and Paul, to Sri Lanka, they adapted favorite songs to the local culture. Everyone contributed.

Video Diary

You know that the video camera can't be beat for bringing the adventure home with you, but how about giving your child the chance to make his own video of the trip? When Sarah Brokaw was twelve and the family took a trip to Africa, Sarah was in charge of making the family film. Years later, the family still enjoys seeing serious Sarah, microphone in hand, reporting on the accommodations, and the animals wandering by, in addition to her family's various comments about the trip.

Have your child act as the reporter. He can record grandparents, the innkeeper, the waiter in the restaurant (not just the beautiful mountains in the distance). He can take wide shots of the scenery and close-ups of Dad asleep in the sun. It's fun to let your child be the director — the result will truly give you an idea of your trip through his eyes. It's only time to stop when you run out of film.

Singing Stars

Not all of your taping needs to be sightseeing-oriented. Have your family "cut a record" (isn't this how the Osmonds started?). Using your audio recorder and some blank tapes, you and your children can perform and record your favorite songs while on the road. If you are really adventurous, you might have your kids try to write their own words to well-known tunes. Everyone can sing different parts and pretend to be different musical instruments. The beauty of this is that you can play it back immediately while you are still traveling. This tape will surely get heavy airtime — getting played and replayed during the trip.

Family Travel Times

In addition to keeping a personal journal, try writing an edition of the *Family Travel Times*. Each member of the family can write small articles about their vacation: how they got there, what they've seen, what they've loved or hated about the weather, the food, the cultural differences. Your kids may even choose to be columnists about certain topics — one can be a restaurant reviewer, another a critic of the driver, or a columnist who writes about his impressions of the people he sees. Be sure to take photographs and draw pictures to accompany your articles.

When you get home, cut and paste your articles and pictures on sheets of 8½-by-11-inch paper. Photocopy these pages, and assemble to hand out to family, friends, and, of course, each person who went on the trip.

QUEEN FOR A DAY.

⭐ You can make or buy funny captions for the pictures in your travelogues.

⭐ Collect your vacation memorabilia: menus, postcards, brochures, ticket stubs, photos, and all the rest. When you return home, make a collage, and frame. It will be a wonderful memento many years later.

⭐ *Maggie Moss Tucker, mom of Jonathan and Jennie, tells us that the Japanese have a proverb that goes something like "To travel is to be educated." The Tuckers visit the local library in Boston to sign out books all about their destination before any trip. By the time they arrive, everyone is an expert at identifying things they have already seen in books.*

Trip Calendar

Draw a calendar of the days your trip covers on a large piece of drawing paper so you can roll it up and carry it on the trip. Each square should be large enough for everyone to write an observation of the day. If you know in advance, fill in details of where you will be or what you will be doing each day. As the trip progresses, jot down strange or particularly funny things that happened, changes in plans (it will be interesting to see how closely you stayed to your original schedule), a new discovery to remember, how many miles you covered that day. The calendar will also be valuable for the kids to see how far they have come during the trip and how much time is left. It may make those last days especially precious since they will be able to see that the trip will soon end and they will be home.

GLUE PHOTO TO POSTER BOARD —

F R O N T

Dear Jane Helen is coming on Sunday Love, Joe

To Jane Jones Main Street MV NH 03092

B A C K

VACATION / JULY

Sunday	Monday	Tuesday	Wednesday	Thursday	Friday	Saturday
	1	2	3	4	5	6
7 To the beach	8 Went sailing	9 ALL DAY	10 SUNNY AGAIN	11 Climbed Mt. Wona	12 FISHED	13 stayed at camp
14 Saw an owl	15 ATE LOTS OF Watermelon	16 DRIVE to Joe's	17 Ate 6 hot dogs	18 Saw a snake	19 I LOVE THE WOODS	20 scraped my knee OUCH!
21 THUNDER	22 I GOT STUNG BY A BEE	23 BEACH	24 Home	25	26	27
28	29	30	31			

Picture Postcards

When you get home, turn some of your photos from the trip into postcards. Cut out poster board (any color light enough to write on — try the new neons!!) in the same size as the photo. Cut out a piece of sticky photo-mounting paper in the same size. Insert the photo-mount paper between the poster board and the photo and press with a warm iron. Hold for about 10 seconds. Draw a border around the poster board with a line separating the address from the message section.

Use these postcards for corresponding with friends you've made or family you've visited. You can also save them as mementos of the trip.

Moving Around

Travel Exercise Program

Long periods of driving are often tedious and frustrating for kids. Getting up and moving around is crucial, whether you've been sitting in a car, on an airplane, or in a train car. Doing some simple exercises as often as possible not only will keep your body in shape but will diminish the chances of kids getting bored and increase the likelihood of their being happy travelers. Kids as young as 3 years old can do these exercises. You can do some of them while you are sitting in the car, in the train, or on the plane, some standing in the back of an airplane, and all of them when you stop the car to get out and move around.

Plan to stop at least every two hours, more often if you're not in a hurry and you see a park or a playground. Remember to put a Frisbee and/or a ball in your car box. A simple jump rope can be used for:

JUMP ROPE GAMES

Rock the Cradle:

Two people hold the ends of the rope and rock it back and forth instead of revolving it.

Wind the Clock:

While the rope is turning, count from 1 to 12, making a quarter turn clockwise each time. Your child can do this alone or with his parents turning the rope for him.

Square Dancing:

Two players turn the rope while jumpers link arms and do a "Do-si-do," all the while jumping.

Chasing:

This involves two turners and at least two jumpers. The first jumper enters, jumps over the rope once, and then rushes out as the second jumper enters, and so on.

☀ *Carry small plastic resealable bags for small toys, supplies, and garbage.*

Hopping:

Two players turn as the jumper rushes in and hops, alternating legs for each turn of the rope. After 10 hops, the jumper runs out and is replaced by another jumper.

Visiting:

One player starts jumping alone, turning her own rope. Another player jumps in and faces her, "visiting" for a while before jumping out again.

★ Dress in layers when traveling. You will always be prepared for being too cool or too hot.

PLAYGROUND GAMES

If you have a little more time, or after you have finished your picnic lunch, you can play a mini softball game or hopscotch, or try playing "Box Baseball" and "Hit the Coin" for some fun exercise.

Box Baseball:

This game is played across three squares (each approximately 4 feet by 4 feet) that you can sketch on pavement with chalk (see drawing). Player 1 is the California Angels and Player 2 is the New York Yankees. Player 1 throws the ball into Player 2's box, passing it over the strikeout area. Player 2, standing outside of his box, tries to catch the ball after one bounce. If he succeeds, it counts as an out for the Angels. But if he doesn't catch the ball after one bounce, each additional bounce means one more base for the Angels — so that two bounces mean a single; three bounces, a double; four bounces, a triple; and five bounces, a home run. If Player 1's throw bounces into the strike area, or misses Player 2's box, it's "strike one," and he must throw again. Three strikes make an out, and it's Player 2's turn to throw. After nine innings, the player with the higher score wins.

★ Have the young travelers put one another through the paces. Let them take turns calling out exercises that everyone must follow. Ten jumping jacks. Five squats. Twelve push-ups.

Hit the Coin:

Your will need two players, your ball, a coin, chalk, and a paved surface. Place a coin on the crack between squares in the sidewalk. Or draw two boxes, each 5 feet square, and separate them with a straight line. One player stands in each box. The object is to bounce the ball on the coin (try to really stretch your arms as you reach for the ball), which scores one point. If your ball flips the coin over, you get two points and the chance to put the coin back on the dividing line, in case it has been knocked away from you. If you miss the coin completely, you continue to take turns bouncing the ball until someone scores a hit. The first player to reach a score of 21 wins.

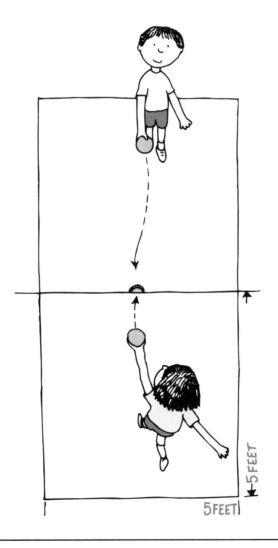

5 FEET

5FEET

☀ "It's going to happen. Sometime, somewhere, it will happen." That's Hildy Gottlieb Hill explaining how she found what she considers to be the cleverest solution to a terrible problem. "We were just taking off on the plane to New York. Joanna was only a little over a year old and had drunk a lot of milk, and suddenly vomited all over me and all over the seats in front of us. I could barely move, could hardly clean everything up, and the stench was the worst thing I had ever smelled. As I was frantically trying to imagine spending the next five hours with this smell (and trying not to imagine how the other passengers must have felt), the stewardess came by holding a large bag of coffee grinds in her hands and proceeded to spill the grinds all over the area that had been hit by Joanna. Instantly, everything smelled of fresh-brewed coffee!"

Stretching Exercises for Car and Plane

REACH FOR THE STARS

This exercise works your shoulders and is a good overall stretch. It may be done while seated in the car, train, or airplane, or standing on the side of the road or in the back of the plane. Stretch for the sky with one arm and "grab a star"; then reach with the other arm. This can also be done with both arms raised high overhead. If you sway like a tree from side to side, you will stretch the obliques (the muscles on the sides of your body). Repeat three times.

⭐ When Elaine Mercer took her granddaughter, Joprin Chiffy, to Florida for their vacation, the flight was so turbulent that the passengers were quite unnerved, with the exception of Joprin, who exclaimed, "That was great! Can we do it again?"

I DON'T KNOW

This exercise works your shoulders and may be done sitting in your seat or standing in place. Shrug your shoulders as if to indicate you don't know something. Repeat three times.

AIRPLANE

This exercise stretches your sides (obliques) and may be done while seated or standing on the floor (but you can't have someone standing or sitting right next to you or you'll hit them with your arms). With your arms straight out to your sides, lean to the left and lean to the right. Repeat three times.

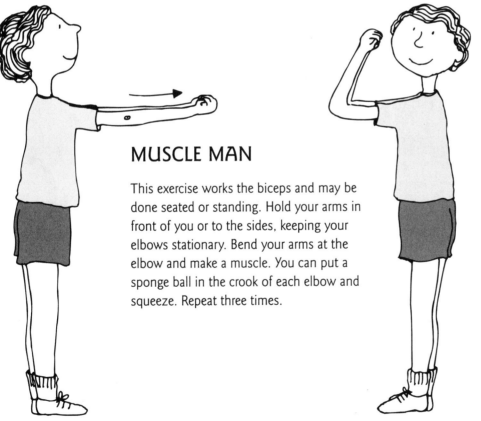

MUSCLE MAN

This exercise works the biceps and may be done seated or standing. Hold your arms in front of you or to the sides, keeping your elbows stationary. Bend your arms at the elbow and make a muscle. You can put a sponge ball in the crook of each elbow and squeeze. Repeat three times.

★ *If you have more than one child, try wearing the same color shirts or hats so you can see each other in a crowd.*

107

These additional exercises – from Nancy Lynch, who is the fitness and aquatics director of Hampshire Hills Sports and Fitness Club in Milford, New Hampshire – are particularly effective for the crowd in the backseat or on a train or plane.

Shoulders:

Sitting forward on your seat, clasp your hands behind your back, palms down, and press them down, lifting your shoulders up toward the ceiling.

When brunettes Jodi and Elizabeth Guber were kids, they loved to go to Mexico for winter vacations and soak up the sun. Mom Lynda, a bright and freckled redhead who stayed out of the sun all her life, tried to teach the girls to wear hats on all their beachside vacations. It seemed like a losing battle until she warned her daughters, "If you don't, the sun will make your hair look just like mine."

Neck:

Pull your shoulders straight down and lift your chest and face upward, keeping your shoulders pulled down. Now bring the right ear to the right shoulder and then to the center. Repeat on the left side. Another neck exercise is to slowly look out the right window, look at your lap, and then slowly look out the left window.

Side Stretches:

With one hand pressed on the seat, reach toward the roof of the car with the other hand. Switch sides. An alternate exercise is to clasp your hands pressing up toward the ceiling.

Torso Stretches:

Place your right hand on the outside of the left thigh. Turn at the waist to the left, not moving the rest of your body, and look out the left window. Repeat with your left hand on the right thigh and look toward the right.

Back:

Place your hands on your knees and bend over from your hips with your back flat, head up, and chest forward. Press your nose to the seat in front of you.

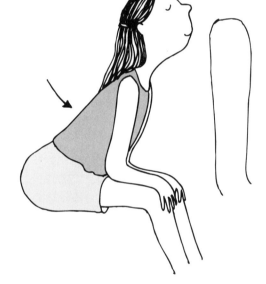

Meredith's Grandmother Harvey kept a pillow handy for grandchildren to hold on their stomachs when they were carsick. "It settles the tummy," she claimed, and it does seem to work!

Upper Back:

Hold on to the sides of the seat in front of you and lean back, head up, shoulders relaxed.

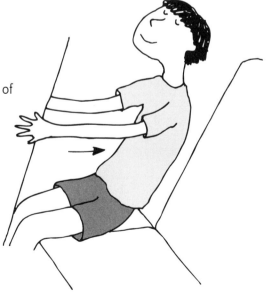

When, Jill Weber moved from New York to New Hampshire, she would return periodically for work to New York. By the time son Remy was 3, he had begun to join his mom on her trips. Jill, fearful that she might lose Remy in the big New York crowds, included in his backpack a list of emergency numbers in New York — the office she would be using, her best friend's home and office, etc. Remy never got lost, but the emergency list sure made an impression on him. He is now 19, and every time he packs, he includes a list of his very own emergency numbers.

A tip from Paddy Calistro: Her kids, Genevieve and David McAuley, always wear slip-on shoes while traveling in the car. They are easy to take off during the ride and put back on before they jump out of the car for a break.

Shoulders and Sides:
Moving only from the waist, reach first for one door. Sit up straight and then reach all the way over toward the other door.

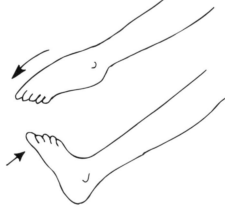

Hands:
Make a fist and open your hands wide. Wiggle those fingers!

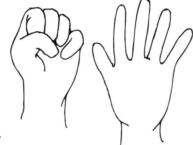

Legs:
Point your toes and then pull them back toward your face.

Toes:
Take off those shoes and wiggle those toes.

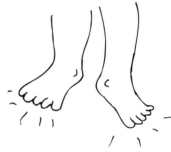

110

Stretches First Thing out of the Car

⭐ *Take your children on a mini nature hike when you stop at a park for a well-deserved afternoon stretch. They may add their discoveries to their "Nature Walk Diary" (see page 96).*

1. Put your hands on top of your bottom, slightly arching your back by tilting your upper body back and pushing the front of your legs forward. This counters the position your body has been in while riding in the car.

2. Reach for the trees, gently swaying from side to side, stretching your torso.

3. Go to the nearest bench and place the heel of your foot on the bench seat. Now stretch the backs of your legs. Have someone stand behind you if you think you might fall.

THE SODA CAN WORKOUT

With a soda can in each hand:

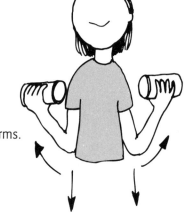

Biceps:

With elbows close to the side, raise and lower the forearms.

Chest and Shoulders:

Press your hands out in front.

Shoulders:

Press your hands straight overhead.

Calf Raises:

While sitting, rest your hands on top of your knees. Now raise and lower your legs.

Quads:

Holding a can between your knees, raise and lower your legs.

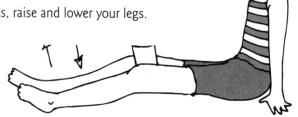

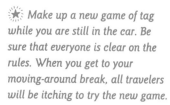

⁂ Make up a new game of tag while you are still in the car. Be sure that everyone is clear on the rules. When you get to your moving-around break, all travelers will be itching to try the new game.

Road Food

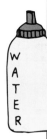

H ow about a picnic instead of stopping for lunch or snacks at a restaurant? Our Road Food recipes will make your roadside picnics special — they are easy to make and delicious to eat. Make life as easy for yourself as possible when you're on the road. Know the pitfalls ahead of time (not all of the hazards are due to highway construction!):

★ Salty foods make kids thirsty, so eat them in moderation. To cut down on thirst, carry water in the car. Small thermos or plastic "sippers" are perfect so every traveler can have his own supply.

★ Drinks come in a variety of containers. Boxed drinks with straws are good because they are easily handled and disposed of, and the straws minimize spillage. (If you've got little kids, there are rigid plastic holders that minimize squirting and squeezing.) One of the best solutions for liquids is the squeeze bottles popular with runners and bikers.

★ To save on space, buy collapsible drinking cups and mark with everyone's initials for identification.

★ Use an empty cardboard six-pack drink box for holding unfinished drinks, empty bottles, or cans.

★ Bring plastic utensils.

★ A Swiss Army or pocket knife is a must.

★ A roll of paper towels for the car.

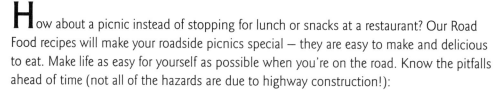

★ A bottle opener.

★ In warm weather, freeze your bread the night before traveling. In the morning, take out the number of slices you need, spread with your choice of filling, and then wrap. The bread will work as an insulator and will thaw out by lunchtime.

★ You can freeze a small can of juice before packing it in a lunch box. The can will keep everything else in the lunch box cool and will itself thaw out so your child can then drink the juice. If you're using a paper lunch bag, be sure to insert the can into a plastic bag first, or it will sweat as it thaws out and destroy the bag.

★ Frozen Blue Ice bags, which can be purchased at the supermarket or hardware store, are especially handy to use in a cooler or lunch box.

★ Insulated lunch boxes or coolers will work much better than paper bags, especially in warm weather.

★ Keep a container of disposable wipes handy. Put them next to the food supply.

★ Road food always needs to be easy to transport and clean up. Popcorn or tortilla chips are guaranteed to fall down beneath the seat cushions or into the transmission box — try keeping those snacks for roadside eating.

★ Keep all car food together in one location (such as a cooler). Make use of individual container boxes and reclosable plastic bags for easy organizing. Load the container according to your family's tastes.

★ Core small whole apples and fill them with peanut butter and raisins. Sliced and peeled apples in small plastic bags are ideal toddler snacks. Sprinkling the apples with lemon juice will keep them from turning brown. Any fruit in season such as pears, plums, bananas, or grapes would be good additions to your supply.

★ Dried fruits such as raisins, cherries, apples, papaya, bananas, apricots, pears, and cranberries won't bruise or spoil on long trips.

✷ Things to fill with salads, sliced cheeses, and meats:
> *won tons*
> *pitas*
> *empanadas*
> *tortillas*
> *apples*
> *lettuce leaves*
> *crescent rolls*
> *snow peas*
> *baked potato skins*

★ Cut celery and carrots into sticks. Pack in plastic containers and add several ice cubes. This will keep them cool and crisp. Other popular vegetables for snacking include green, red, or yellow pepper slices, cauliflower, snow peas, peas, and raw string beans.

★ Peanut butter, the universal kid food, is nutritious, filling, and, with a little care, not *too* messy! Sporting goods stores stock little tubes that can be filled with peanut butter (squeeze directly onto firm crackers that don't break easily or noncrumbly bread such as pita or bagels).

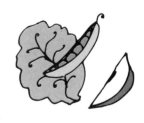

★ Cube, slice, or roll pieces of cheese (string cheese is great). Add crackers for a nutritious, filling snack.

★ Buy a container of soft cheese such as Boursin or a goat cheese to use for a dip. Guacamole, hummus, and tahini also come ready to serve in plastic containers and are available in most markets. Dip into these with your vegetables, crackers, chips, or pita bread.

Creative Packing Hints

★ Pack lunches in plastic bags and close with funny stickers.

☀ *Store a roll of large plastic bags in your cooler. These will come in handy for trash, wet bathing suits or shoes, dirty diapers, or mementos collected along the way.*

★ Include funny messages in individually packed sandwiches.

★ Buy a bag of fortune cookies. You can give them out at each stop and have everyone do a dramatic reading of their fortune.

☀ *Store cheddar fish, raisins, pumpkin seeds, granola, and other small snacking foods in plastic margarine containers or compartmentalized bead holders.*

★ Cut traditional sandwiches with cookie cutters to surprise tired and cranky travelers. You can also cut a sandwich into the shape of your child's initials.

★ Pack some comics or jokes you cut out of newspapers or magazines. They will be a great comic relief on long car rides.

Recipe Ideas

AMBROSIA

5 large oranges, peeled
4 medium bananas, sliced
¼ cup fresh orange juice
½ cup sugar
¾ cup flaked unsweetened
    shredded coconut

Be sure to remove all the white pith and the membrane when peeling the oranges. Section the oranges or cut them into pieces. Mix with the bananas. Add the orange juice at once. Combine the sugar and coconut; add to the fruit and toss gently.

Place in a sealed plastic container or sturdy plastic bag and keep chilled in a cooler.

SERVES 6

IN-A-HURRY CHEESE STICKS

3 slices sourdough bread,
    crusts removed
Butter or margarine, at room
    temperature
½ cup grated cheddar cheese

Spread the bread slices with butter. Sprinkle the cheese on top. Chill, covered, in the refrigerator overnight. (If you make this in the morning, allow 30 minutes for chilling.) Cut each bread slice into 1-inch-wide strips. Toast both sides in a toaster oven or broiler until browned, 5 to 10 minutes.

Wrap in foil.

MAKES 9 STICKS

BAKED POTATO SKINS

Baking potato, well washed

Preheat oven to 500°F.

Prick a potato and wrap in aluminum foil. Bake for 45 minutes or until soft. Remove from oven. (To bake a potato in a microwave oven, prick potato and place in oven on a microwave-safe plate. Cook on high for 10 minutes.) Cut potato in half and scoop out insides, leaving skin intact. Return skin to a 400°F oven for 30 minutes. Cool.

Store in a plastic container and refrigerate. Serve with a soft cheese like Boursin or with dips.

PETER'S ROASTED PUMPKIN SEEDS

2 cups hulled raw pumpkin seeds
¼ cup unhulled sesame seeds
2 tablespoons grated Parmesan cheese
1 tablespoon butter or margarine,
    melted
1 tablespoon Worcestershire sauce
Salt

Preheat oven to 375°F.

Combine all ingredients. Spread out the mixture on a baking sheet. Bake for approximately 20 minutes or until lightly toasted. Let cool and season to taste with salt.

Store in a covered plastic container or sturdy plastic bags, and keep in your cooler.

★ Buy applesauce in snack-size containers for an easy treat.

★ Hildy Gottlieb Hill flies cross-country often, taking Joanna, 6, and Miranda, 3½, with her. She always packs the kids' favorite desserts, because the meals are never served fast enough, and giving the kids their favorites puts them in a great mood instantly.

117

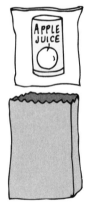

Nancy Perry and her five brothers and sisters grew up in Florida. Her mom, Dorothy, always packed picnic lunches for their car trips, even short ones. "Even today I can't get in a car without smelling the sandwiches in that basket. Eating picnics on the side of the highway is a memory I still cherish!"

CHEESY POPCORN

6 to 8 cups popped popcorn
½ cup (1 stick) margarine,
    at room temperature
½ cup grated cheddar cheese
½ teaspoon salt

Make the popcorn as you normally do. Mix together the margarine, cheese, and salt in a small bowl. Melt on the stovetop or in a microwave. Pour mixture over the popcorn and let cool for a few minutes.

Store individual portions in plastic sandwich bags.

MAKES 4 SERVINGS

SESAME COCONUT BARS

3 cups sesame seeds
1 cup unsweetened shredded coconut
2 tablespoons peanut butter, softened
2 tablespoons honey
½ teaspoon salt
¼ teaspoon vanilla extract

Preheat oven to 300°F. Butter or spray a large baking sheet with cooking spray.

Mix together all ingredients. (As you mix, the mixture will seem dry — but don't add water – it's really O.K.!) Empty onto the prepared pan and press the mixture down evenly. Bake for about 30 minutes, or until browned (watch carefully to make sure the mixture doesn't burn). Let cool and cut into bars.

Wrap the bars individually in plastic wrap or store in a covered plastic container or sturdy plastic bags.

MAKES ABOUT 8 BARS

TRAIL COOKIES

½ cup vegetable oil, plus extra
    for greasing baking sheet
½ cup applesauce
2 egg whites
½ cup frozen apple juice
    concentrate, thawed
1 cup granola (any variety, or see
    our recipe, opposite page)
½ cup all-purpose flour
⅓ cup whole-wheat flour
1 teaspoon ground cinnamon
1 teaspoon ground allspice
1 teaspoon ground ginger
1 tablespoon minced crystallized ginger
½ teaspoon ground cloves
1 cup currants or raisins
¾ cup packed brown sugar
2 tablespoons fresh orange juice
2 tablespoons fresh lemon juice
3 cups "quick" oatmeal
1 teaspoon baking soda
3 teaspoons vanilla extract

Preheat oven to 350°F. Lightly wipe a large baking sheet with vegetable oil.

Combine all the ingredients in a large bowl and mix well. Place ¼-cup measures of the cookie dough on the sheet, 2 inches apart. Press the dough into large circles. Bake for 15 minutes, or until golden brown. Let the cookies cool on the sheet for about 1 minute, then remove them and let them cool completely on a rack. These are fragile and soft when still warm and firm up as they cool.

MAKES APPROXIMATELY 3 DOZEN
MEDIUM-SIZE COOKIES

CINNAMON SQUARES

6 tablespoons (¾ stick) margarine
½ teaspoon ground cinnamon
⅛ teaspoon ground nutmeg
3 cups spoon-size Shredded Wheat

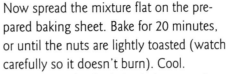

Melt the margarine in a large skillet over moderate heat. Stir in the cinnamon and nutmeg. Add the Shredded Wheat and toss to coat. Cook for approximately 5 minutes, or until lightly browned. Stir frequently. Drain on paper towels. Refrigerate for 5 to 10 minutes.

Store individual snack portions in plastic sandwich bags or small plastic containers.

PEANUT MIX

1¼ cups peanuts
¾ cup soy nuts
1 cup raw hulled sunflower seeds
1 cup pumpkin seeds
4 teaspoons safflower oil
2 tablespoons peanut oil
2 teaspoons light soy sauce
1 teaspoon sugar
½ teaspoon salt
¼ teaspoon ground ginger
2 pinches of garlic powder

Preheat the oven to 300°F .

Spray a baking sheet with vegetable spray. Combine the peanuts, soy nuts, and sunflower and pumpkin seeds. Pour the safflower and peanut oils and all of the seasonings into a blender and mix on low speed for 5 seconds. Pour over the peanut-and-seed mixture. Toss to coat completely.

Now spread the mixture flat on the prepared baking sheet. Bake for 20 minutes, or until the nuts are lightly toasted (watch carefully so it doesn't burn). Cool.

Store in individual plastic bags or a large plastic container.

MAKES APPROXIMATELY 4 CUPS OF MIX

TOM'S GRANOLA

4 cups old-fashioned oats
1 cup unsweetened shredded coconut
⅓ cup sesame seeds
1 cup wheat germ
½ cup safflower oil
½ cup honey
3 cups mixed nuts, such as slivered
*   almonds, walnuts, and pine nuts*
2 to 3 cups dried cherries

Preheat oven to 300°F .

Combine the oats, coconut, sesame seeds, and wheat germ in a large heatproof bowl. In a medium saucepan, warm the oil and honey until bubbly. Pour the warm honey-and-oil mixture onto the oat mixture and stir to coat. Add the nuts. Spread the entire mixture over shallow baking pans. Bake, stirring frequently, for about 25 minutes, or until golden brown. Remove from oven and let cool. Stir in the dried cherries. That's it!

Store in individual plastic bags. Great as an alternative to a fast-food breakfast, as well.

MAKES APPROXIMATELY 8 CUPS OF MIX

★ *Buy granola bars instead of candy bars for car snacks.*

★ *Add M&Ms to your granola when using it as a trail mix.*

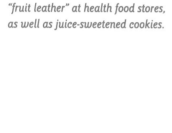

⭐ You can find juice-sweetened "fruit leather" at health food stores, as well as juice-sweetened cookies.

PENNY WHISTLE BANANA BREAD

½ cup (1 stick) butter or margarine, at room temperature

¾ cup packed brown sugar

1 egg

1 cup whole-wheat flour

½ cup unbleached white flour

1 teaspoon baking soda

½ teaspoon salt (optional)

¼ teaspoon ground cinnamon (optional)

2 or 3 ripe bananas

¼ cup buttermilk or plain yogurt

1 cup chopped walnuts or sunflower seeds (optional)

Preheat oven to 350°F. Butter a 9- by 5-inch loaf pan.

In the bowl of an electric mixer, cream the butter with the sugar until the mixture is fluffy and light brown in color. Beat in the egg.

On a sheet of waxed paper, sift together the flours, baking soda, salt, and cinnamon. In a small bowl, combine the bananas and buttermilk or yogurt and stir until well blended. Alternately add the flour mixture and banana mixture to the creamed butter, mixing thoroughly after each addition, and beating until all of the ingredients are thoroughly combined. Fold in the walnuts or sunflower seeds by hand. Pour the batter into the prepared loaf pan and smooth the top. Bake for 50 minutes to 1 hour, or until a toothpick inserted in the center of the loaf comes out clean. Let the bread stand in the pan on a wire rack for at least 15 minutes. Remove from the pan and let sit at room temperature, uncovered, for at least 1 hour. (If you try to cut this bread when it is warm, it will crumble.)

When firm, wrap in plastic wrap or bag individual slices for travel.

CRANBERRY BREAD

1 tablespoon orange rind

¾ cup orange juice

¼ cup butter

1 cup sugar

1 egg

2 cups chopped cranberries

2 cups sifted all-purpose flour

1½ teaspoons baking powder

½ teaspoon baking soda

½ teaspoon salt

1 cup chopped walnuts

Preheat oven to 325°F. Oil 2 loaf pans and line the bottoms with waxed or parchment paper.

Add the grated orange rind to the orange juice, then set aside until needed.

Thoroughly cream the butter, sugar, and egg. Add the cranberries and stir.

Sift together the flour, baking powder, baking soda, and salt. Stir the walnuts into the dry ingredients. Add the dry mix to the batter alternately with the orange juice and stir well. This batter will be quite stiff.

Divide the batter between the two prepared loaf pans. Bake for approximately 1 hour and 15 minutes or until a testing toothpick comes out clean from the center of the loaves. Remove from the pans and cool on a wire rack.

Slice and wrap individual slices in plastic wrap.

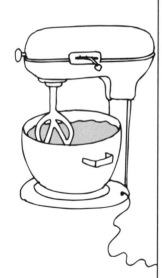

MARC'S JERKY

Pam butter spray
1 pound thinly sliced cooked turkey or
   sliced roast beef
½ cup teriyaki sauce
Hickory salt

Spray a pan with butter spray. Lay slices of cold cuts on pan. Season both sides of meat with teriyaki sauce. Season with hickory salt to taste. Remove cold cuts from pan and bake in a toaster oven at 400°F for 20 minutes. Allow 5 minutes to cool.

   Store in plastic bags.

SWEET POTATO CHIPS

Heat 3 inches of vegetable oil in a wok to 375°F. Peel sweet potatoes and slice them on a slicer or in a food processor to the desired thickness. Fry until crisp. Drain on paper towels. Season with salt, or for a more interesting taste (says Don Ernstein, our friend and caterer of Wonderful Foods in Los Angeles), season with superfine sugar and cinnamon.

PEANUT BUTTER LADYFINGERS

8 dried figs
2 cups smooth peanut butter
4 ladyfingers, chilled

In a food processor or blender, process the figs and peanut butter to a fairly smooth paste. If they are not already precut, slice open 4 ladyfingers. Spread one half with the peanut butter mixture and cover with the other half.

   Wrap in plastic wrap

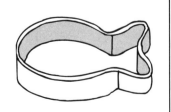

GO FISH

10 slices thinly sliced firm white bread
1 cup chunky peanut butter
¼ cup vegetable oil

Preheat oven to 350°F.
   Trim the crusts from the bread slices and set aside.
   Use a fish-shaped cookie cutter to cut shapes out of the bread. Reserve the scraps. Place the fish flat on a baking sheet. Toast lightly in the oven.
   Place the trimmed crusts and the bread scraps on another baking sheet and bake until golden brown. Place in a food processor or a blender and blend to make fine bread crumbs. Remove the crumbs to a shallow bowl.
   Heat the peanut butter and the oil in a small saucepan until blended and warm. Dip the toasted fish completely into the peanut butter mixture and then coat with the bread crumbs. Let the fish dry flat on a baking sheet.
   Store in an airtight container.

MAKES 10 TO 48 FISH, DEPENDING ON THE SIZE OF YOUR COOKIE CUTTER

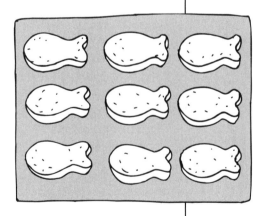

⭐ *Sydny Miner doesn't count on the airline to have kid-appropriate food, even if she's ordered her two boys special meals. She brings lots of drinks (cartons of juice and milk packs are a godsend), nonspoilable sandwiches (as in peanut butter and jelly), individually packaged string cheese sticks or mini-cheeses in wax, and other snacks (try to avoid anything too salty or sugary).*

Says Sydny Miner: "We don't take a long car trip without our cooler. I always store napkins, wipes, condiments, a couple of small bottles of water, a small jar of peanut butter, a squeeze bottle of honey, a couple of juice packs, a bag with a bottle opener and knife and ice packs in it. My kids tend to eat and drink nonstop when confined to the car. Favorite travel foods include: flavored rice cakes, noncrushable fruit, juice-sweetened fruit roll-ups and cookies, the eternal peanut butter and jelly sandwich, carrot and celery sticks, individual packs of dry cereal — nothing too exotic, fatty, salty, or sweet, but all very reassuring."

HUMMUS WITH TAHINI

1 can (15 ounces) garbanzos, drained, liquid reserved
½ cup prepared tahini
3 tablespoons lemon juice
1 large clove garlic
¼ teaspoon ground cumin (optional)
Salt and pepper

Put garbanzos into a blender. Add ¼ cup of the tahini, and the lemon juice, garlic, and cumin. Pour in ¼ cup garbanzo liquid and whirl, starting and stopping motor and adding more liquid, if needed, until mixture is smooth and the consistency of heavy batter. Season to taste with salt and pepper. Place in a plastic container. Press the middle down with the back of a soup spoon and pour in remaining ¼ cup of tahini. Cover with the lid.

Serve at picnic with crudités or pita bread, fresh or toasted.

MAKES ABOUT 1 ½ CUPS

SALSA

3 large, firm tomatoes, coarsely chopped
1 teaspoon minced jalapeño pepper (or to taste)
¼ cup chopped scallions
¼ cup finely chopped cilantro
2 tablespoons finely chopped fresh parsley
1 tablespoon olive oil
2 teaspoons fresh lemon or lime juice

Mix all ingredients in a medium bowl; let stand at room temperature for 2 hours to blend flavors.

Store in a plastic container.

MAKES ABOUT 4 CUPS

JOAN'S COUSCOUS AND CHICK PEA SALAD

1¾ cup water
½ teaspoon salt
1 cup couscous
1 can (15 ounces) chick peas
2 red peppers, diced
4 scallions, chopped
½ cup finely chopped carrots
½ cup diced pitted Kalamata olives
½ cup crumbled feta cheese

MINT VINAIGRETTE

¾ cup mint leaves
3 tablespoons red wine vinegar
1 garlic clove, minced
1 teaspoon Dijon mustard
½ cup olive oil
pinch of sugar

Bring the water and salt to a boil in a medium saucepan. Stir in the couscous. Remove the saucepan from the heat, cover, and let stand 5 minutes. Fluff with a fork. Add the chick peas, red peppers, scallions, carrots, and olives.

Mix the dressing ingredients together in a bowl and pour over the salad, tossing to distribute dressing and vegetables evenly. Gently mix in the feta. Season to taste with salt and pepper.

MAKES 4 TO 6 SERVINGS AS A MAIN COURSE OR MORE IF A SIDE DISH

Roadside Picnics

Roadside picnics or picnics in the park can be trip highlights if they're well organized ahead of time. Don't forget the paper plates, napkins, utensils, and disposable wipes! While younger family members are getting rid of some excess energy, have some crudités with hummus or tortilla chips and salsa ready. Be sure to pack your picnic in a cooler that is easy to transport. The picnics should be easy to set up (especially if everyone serves himself) and a breeze to clean up when it's over.

Here are five picnic plans that can be easily adapted to suit your family's taste. Some recipes need to be prepared at home before the trip begins and so will be good for the first day only. Others require only that the ingredients be in the cooler and combined on the spot.

★ Good only for first picnic or one-day trips

★ ★ Can keep for more than one day

ROADSIDE PICNIC #1

- ★ CHEESE ROLL-UPS
- ★ APPLE CARROT SLAW
- ★ SESAME CHICKEN
- ★ RICE SALAD
- ★★ CARAMEL SQUARES

ROADSIDE PICNIC #2

SANDWICH BOARD:

- ★ COTTAGE CHEESE AND MARMALADE SANDWICH
- ★ TURKEY, BACON, AND APPLE CLUB
- ★ HAM AND SWISS DOUBLE DECKER

- ★ KIM TYLER'S ORIENTAL CHICKEN SALAD
- ★★ CHEWY OATMEAL COOKIES

ROADSIDE PICNIC #3

- ★ SAUSAGE BAGUETTES
- ★ LENTIL SALAD
- ★ GARDEN SALAD
- ★★ MAPLE BARS
- ★ FRUIT KEBABS

ROADSIDE PICNIC #5

- ★ CHICKEN WINGS
- ★ MEAT LOAF SANDWICHES
- ★ ADELE'S POTATO SALAD
- ★ BROCCOLI SALAD
- ★★ CHOCOLATE BARS

ROADSIDE PICNIC #4

SANDWICH BOARD:

- ★ TURKEY AND CRANBERRIES ON PUMPERNICKEL
- ★ SMOKED TURKEY ON RAISIN BREAD
- ★ ROAST BEEF TORTILLAS
- ★ CREAM CHEESE AND CUCUMBER SANDWICH

- ★ JENNY'S PEANUT BUTTER NOODLES
- ★★ BLOND BROWNIES

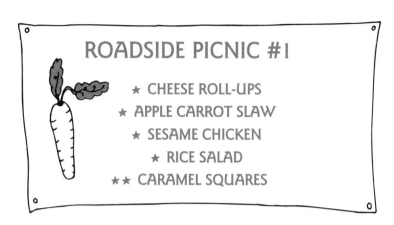

ROADSIDE PICNIC #1

★ CHEESE ROLL-UPS
★ APPLE CARROT SLAW
★ SESAME CHICKEN
★ RICE SALAD
★★ CARAMEL SQUARES

★ Hildy Gottlieb Hill never travels with juice. "The kids want it all the time and drink too much of it, the sugar makes them hyper and everything they touch sticky, and the quantities make them pee all the time. Take water instead!"

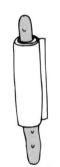

CHEESE ROLL-UPS

Swiss, Monterey Jack, or cheddar cheese slices
Bread sticks

Take cheese slices (it's easiest to use pre-sliced cheese) and wrap around bread sticks. Try other kinds of cheese, if you like, and roll around vegetable sticks (cucumber, carrot, celery, or zucchini) as well.

SESAME CHICKEN

6 chicken pieces (fresh, not frozen)
Dash of seasoned salt
Dash of pepper
Dash of paprika
¼ cup sesame seeds
1 cup all-purpose flour
Safflower or peanut oil, for frying

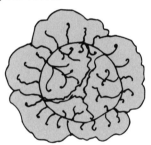

Wash and dry the chicken pieces. Place the salt, pepper, paprika, sesame seeds, and flour in a paper or plastic bag. Drop 2 to 3 chicken pieces into the bag and shake well, until the chicken is completely coated. Heat oil (3 inches deep) in a deep fryer or chicken fryer, making sure the oil is very hot before you start cooking. Put in 3 pieces of chicken at a time and cook, uncovered, until golden brown on all sides (a breast takes about 15 minutes, so judge

accordingly). Remove the chicken from the fryer and drain on paper towels.

Store in a plastic container and chill. Keep in your cooler.

APPLE CARROT SLAW

2 cups shredded cabbage
1 cup shredded carrots
1 medium apple, cored and cubed
½ cup mayonnaise
1 teaspoon sugar
½ teaspoon salt
Dash of cinnamon

In a medium plastic bowl, toss the cabbage, carrots, apple, and mayonnaise until well blended. Season with the sugar, salt, and cinnamon. Mix well.

Cover and chill in your cooler until ready to serve.

MAKES 4 SERVINGS

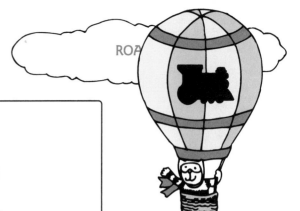

RICE SALAD

2 cups uncooked brown rice
⅓ cup peanut oil
3 tablespoons Asian sesame oil
½ cup orange juice
1 medium clove garlic, crushed
2 tablespoons soy sauce
1 teaspoon salt
1 tablespoon packed brown sugar
2 tablespoons cider vinegar
1 cup chopped fresh or canned
    pineapple
2 scallions, minced
1 stalk celery, finely chopped
½ pound bean sprouts
½ cup raisins
½ cup peanuts, chopped
1 tablespoon sesame seeds
1 cup bell pepper, chopped
1 cup water chestnuts, thinly sliced

Cook rice according to package instructions. Mix together the peanut oil, sesame
oil, orange juice, garlic, soy sauce, salt,
brown sugar, vinegar, and pineapple in a
large bowl. Add the cooked rice and toss
well. Toss in the scallions, celery, bean
sprouts, raisins, peanuts, sesame seeds,
bell pepper, and water chestnuts.

   Store in a plastic container and chill in
your cooler.

MAKES 8 SERVINGS

CARAMEL SQUARES

1 stick butter
1 cup packed brown sugar
1 egg
1 cup sifted all-purpose flour
1 teaspoon baking powder
Pinch of salt
1 teaspoon vanilla
1⅓ cups nuts

Preheat oven to 350°F. Grease a 9- by 9-
inch pan.

   Melt butter and sugar in saucepan over
low heat. Stir until mixture is very smooth.
Cool. Mix in the unbeaten egg. Sift in
flour, baking powder, and salt. Stir in
vanilla and nuts until smooth. Bake 30 to
40 minutes. Cool and cut into squares.

   Store in a plastic container or in individual plastic bags.

MAKES ABOUT 36 SMALL SQUARES

FLOUR

☀ *Bring breakfast-type food, just
in case you and your kids are
awake before the restaurant is
open. You can always stop for a
late-morning snack.*

ROADSIDE PICNIC #2

SANDWICH BOARD:
- ★ COTTAGE CHEESE AND MARMALADE SANDWICH
- ★ TURKEY, BACON, AND APPLE CLUB
- ★ HAM AND SWISS DOUBLE DECKER

- ★ KIM TYLER'S ORIENTAL CHICKEN SALAD
- ★★ CHEWY OATMEAL COOKIES

☀ *Be flexible about junk food, even if you normally don't allow it at home.*

COTTAGE CHEESE AND MARMALADE SANDWICH

1 teaspoon orange marmalade
2 slices egg bread or sourdough bread
¼ cup low-fat cottage cheese

Spread marmalade on one slice of bread. Top with cottage cheese. Close sandwich with other slice of bread.
   Wrap, and store in cooler.

MAKES 1 SANDWICH

TURKEY, BACON, AND APPLE CLUB

1 apple, cored and sliced
4 lettuce leaves, well washed
½ pound smoked turkey, sliced
¼ pound bacon, cooked and drained
8 slices pumpernickel bread
Champagne or honey mustard

Assemble apple slices, lettuce leaf, turkey, and bacon on slice of pumpernickel. Spread with mustard and top with another slice of bread.
   Wrap and store in cooler.

MAKES 4 SANDWICHES

HAM AND SWISS DOUBLE DECKER

Champagne mustard
3 slices whole-wheat bread
2 slices baked ham
2 slices Swiss cheese
2 leaves red lettuce
2 slices tomato
Dill pickle slices
2 slices red onion (optional)

Spread mustard on one slice of bread. Put one slice ham, one slice cheese, one lettuce leaf, one slice tomato, dill pickle slices, and a slice of red onion on the slice of bread. Top with another slice of bread. Repeat. Cut sandwich in four pieces.
   Wrap and store in cooler.

MAKES 1 SANDWICH

RO

KIM TYLER'S ORIENTAL CHICKEN SALAD

2 cups bow tie pasta or other shape
2 cups diced cooked chicken
½ cup diced cucumber
½ head Chinese chopped cabbage
1 small red bell pepper, diced
4 scallions, sliced
½ cup peanut butter
¼ cup rice wine vinegar
3 tablespoons soy sauce
2 tablespoons honey
1 tablespoon Asian sesame oil
Cayenne pepper, optional
½ cup dry-roasted unsalted peanuts

Cook pasta. Drain and rinse with cold water. Combine pasta, chicken, cucumber, cabbage, pepper, and scallions. Toss well. In a separate bowl, mix until smooth the peanut butter, vinegar, soy sauce, honey, and sesame oil. Add cayenne if using. Pour over salad, add peanuts, and toss well.

MAKES 4 SERVINGS

CHEWY OATMEAL COOKIES

1¼ cups (2½ *sticks*) butter
1 cup packed brown sugar
1 cup granulated sugar
2 eggs
1 teaspoon vanilla extract
½ teaspoon salt
1 teaspoon ground nutmeg
1 cup unsweetened shredded coconut
2½ cups rolled oats
1 teaspoon baking soda
1¼ cups unbleached flour

Preheat oven to 350°F.

Thoroughly cream the butter and sugars. Whip in the eggs until the mixture is light. Add the vanilla, salt, and nutmeg and stir. Add the coconut and oats, and blend. Let the dough rest a few minutes. Add the baking soda, and gradually incorporate the flour into the mixture. Drop by spoonfuls onto a greased baking sheet. Bake for approximately 10 to 12 minutes.

Store in a plastic container or individual plastic bags.

MAKES APPROXIMATELY
3 DOZEN COOKIES

★ *Favorite fillings for Pita Pockets:*

★ *sliced turkey with shredded cheddar cheese, slices of red or green pepper, and a teaspoon of chutney*

★ *sliced avocado, crumbled bacon, shredded mozzarella cheese*

★ *falafel balls, hummus, chopped tomatoes, shredded lettuce, and slices of pickles*

★ *cream cheese, slices of roast beef, chopped scallions, and chopped tomatoes*

★ *chopped pineapple, slivers of ham or smoked turkey, and honey mustard*

★ *slices of ham, cheddar cheese, and pickle and Dijon mustard*

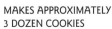

127

ROADSIDE PICNIC #3

★ SAUSAGE BAGUETTES
★ LENTIL SALAD
★ GARDEN SALAD
★ ★ MAPLE BARS
★ FRUIT KEBABS

★ *Mathea Falco always carries nibbles with her to the restaurant so her child can eat something before the food arrives. Ben likes apple slices and apple juice.*

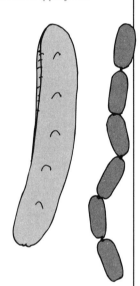

SAUSAGE BAGUETTES

4 (10- to 12-inch) French bread baguettes
1½ pounds Italian sausage, casings removed
1 medium onion, chopped coarsely
1 green or red bell pepper, diced
2 tablespoons vegetable oil
½ cup Dijon mustard
½ cup chopped fresh parsley
Freshly ground black pepper
4 tablespoons (½ stick) butter, melted

Preheat oven to 350°F.

Slice the loaves of French bread in half lengthwise. Scoop out the centers of the loaves. (To make bread crumbs for use later, place in a blender or a food processor. Process until fine bread crumbs have formed. Bake the crumbs in the oven for 10 to 15 minutes, or until golden.)

Reset oven to 450°F. In a large skillet over medium heat, sauté the Italian sausage, onion, and bell pepper until the sausage is brown and crumbly and the onion and bell pepper are soft. Remove from heat and drain off all but 1 tablespoon of fat. Add the vegetable oil, mustard, and parsley, and pepper to taste. Stuff the mixture into the loaves. Brush with melted butter, wrap in foil, and bake for 15 minutes. Remove the foil and continue to bake for a few minutes.

Rewrap in foil and store in your cooler.

MAKES 4 SANDWICHES

LENTIL SALAD

1 pound dried lentils
6 cups water
1 teaspoon salt
2 scallions, with tops, chopped
½ red bell pepper, finely chopped
½ yellow bell pepper, finely chopped
½ green bell pepper, finely chopped
½ cup minced parsley

LEMON DRESSING

¼ cup olive oil
½ tablespoon fresh lemon juice
1 teaspoon Dijon mustard
2 tablespoons fresh basil or 1 teaspoon dried
Salt and pepper to taste

Simmer the lentils in the water with the salt for about 30 minutes, or until tender. Cool and drain. Stir in the scallions, red bell pepper, yellow bell pepper, green bell pepper, and parsley. Store in a plastic container.

Prepare Lemon Dressing: Mix olive oil, lemon juice, mustard, basil, and salt and pepper in a small bowl. Store dressing in a small plastic container.

Keep salad and dressing in your cooler. When ready to serve, toss salad with dressing and adjust seasoning.

SERVES 8

GARDEN SALAD

1 tablespoon raisins

1 tablespoon hulled sunflower seeds

1 tablespoon peanuts

1 tablespoon Lemon Dressing
   (see Lentil Salad, opposite page)

½ tablespoon light soy sauce

2 cups each of shredded carrots,
   spinach, red onions, watercress,
   and red peppers

Salt and pepper to taste

Mix all ingredients in a plastic container and cover. Keep chilled in cooler until ready to serve.

MAPLE BARS

1 12-ounce box brown sugar

1 cup all-purpose flour, unsifted

1 teaspoon baking powder

4 large eggs

Pinch of salt

1 teaspoon maple flavoring

1 cup chopped pecans

Preheat oven to 375°F.

Grease and flour a 9- by 13- by 2-inch pan. Mix brown sugar, flour, and baking powder in a bowl. Add unbeaten eggs, salt, and maple flavoring, and mix well. Stir in pecans. Pour mixture into pan and bake for 20 minutes, or until the middle is set but not hard. Do not overcook. Cool 10 to 15 minutes in pan.

Cut in squares and store in a covered tin so bars remain chewy.

Variation: Vanilla may be used instead of maple flavoring.

MAKES APPROXIMATELY 1 DOZEN BARS,
3 BY 4 INCHES

FRUIT KEBABS

Choose several fruits such as:

   1 banana, sliced thick

   Pineapple chunks

   Seedless or seeded grapes

   Pitted sweet cherries

   Melon pieces or balls

   Orange sections

   Strawberries

   Grapefruit sections

   Papaya pieces

   Kiwi fruit slices

   Peach chunks

   Pear pieces

The quantity of fruit you need will depend on the number of people to be served. We usually figure 12 pieces, or 2 skewers, per person. Thread the fruits on skewers — long bamboo ones are appropriate. If using bananas, peaches, or pears, sprinkle with a little lemon or orange juice. For a variation, roll kebabs in grated coconut.

Keep the kebabs chilled in your cooler.

☆ *A nutritious, filling snack or lunch is the quick-and-easy Apple-Vegetable Pita. Prepare the pitas for a day-trip lunch or the first day of a longer trip and keep in a cooler.*

¼ cup chopped peeled apples
   (dipped in lemon juice)

¼ cup chopped or grated carrot

3 tablespoons chopped celery
   (optional)

1 tablespoon chopped parsley

2 tablespoons chopped cooked
   broccoli

2 tablespoons chopped seeded
   cucumber

1 tablespoon chopped onion

3 tablespoons chopped zucchini

2 tablespoons mayonnaise or plain
   yogurt

1 pita bread

In a bowl, mix together everything but the bread. (You can substitute or add any vegetables.)

Slice open one end of the pita bread and fill the pocket with the mixture. Wrap in plastic wrap.

ROADSIDE PICNIC #4

SANDWICH BOARD:

★ TURKEY AND CRANBERRIES ON PUMPERNICKEL
★ SMOKED TURKEY ON RAISIN BREAD
★ ROAST BEEF TORTILLAS
★ CREAM CHEESE AND CUCUMBER SANDWICH

★ JENNY'S PEANUT BUTTER NOODLES
★★ BLOND BROWNIES

TURKEY AND CRANBERRIES ON PUMPERNICKEL

2 tablespoons cream cheese, softened
2 slices whole-wheat bread
2 cold turkey slices
2 tablespoons cranberry sauce

Spread cream cheese on one slice of whole-wheat bread. Layer turkey slices on top. Cover with the other slice of bread. Wrap sandwich.

Store sandwich and cranberry sauce in cooler. At the picnic, add the cranberry sauce.

MAKES 1 SANDWICH

SMOKED TURKEY ON RAISIN BREAD

2 slices raisin bread
1 tablespoon mustard
2 tablespoons nonfat plain yogurt
⅛ cup cucumber, peeled and thinly sliced
2 slices smoked turkey breast

Spread one slice of bread with the mustard and the yogurt. Layer cucumber slices and turkey slices. Top with remaining bread. Cut in half.

Wrap and store in cooler until ready to eat.

MAKES 1 SANDWICH

ROAST BEEF TORTILLAS

⅓ cup mayonnaise
1 tablespoon prepared horseradish, or more to taste
1 flour or corn tortilla
8 ounces thinly sliced roast beef
Tomato slices
Red onion slices
⅔ cup alfalfa sprouts

In a small bowl, combine the mayonnaise and horseradish. Spread the mixture onto the tortilla, leaving a ½-inch border around the edges. Cover with the slices of roast beef, tomato, and red onion. Sprinkle with alfalfa sprouts. Roll the sandwich tight, jelly-roll-fashion.

Wrap securely in plastic wrap and store in your cooler until ready to serve.

MAKES 1 SANDWICH

CREAM CHEESE AND CUCUMBER SANDWICH

2 tablespoons cream cheese, softened

2 slices pumpernickel bread

¼ cup cucumber, peeled and sliced

Coarsely ground black pepper and salt, to taste

Spread cream cheese on one slice of bread. Top with sliced cucumbers and season to taste with salt and pepper. Close sandwich with the other slice of bread.

Wrap and store in cooler until ready to serve.

MAKES 1 SANDWICH

JENNY'S PEANUT BUTTER NOODLES

1 package (8 ounces) linguine

2 to 3 tablespoons peanut butter

½ teaspoon salt

2 tablespoons soy sauce

1 tablespoon Asian sesame oil

1 teaspoon sugar

½ teaspoon white wine vinegar

2 garlic cloves, crushed

1 teaspoon grated onion

Cook the linguine according to the directions on the package. Drain.

In a large bowl, mix all of the remaining ingredients together. Add linguine to sauce and toss to coat well.

When ready to pack the lunch, put each portion in a small container, cover, and store in the cooler.

MAKES 4 TO 6 SERVINGS

BLOND BROWNIES

1 cup (2 sticks) butter, at room temperature

1 cup all-purpose flour

1 cup granulated sugar

1 cup packed brown sugar

1 tablespoon baking powder

2 eggs

Pinch of salt

½ cup coarsely chopped walnuts

¼ cup (4 ounces) chocolate bits or mini chips

Confectioners' sugar

Preheat oven to 375°F. Butter a 9- by 12-inch glass baking dish or a jelly-roll pan.

In the bowl of an electric mixer, cream together the butter, flour, and granulated sugar until fluffy. Add the brown sugar, baking powder, eggs, and salt, and beat until well mixed. Fold in the walnuts by hand.

Spread the batter in the prepared pan. Sprinkle the chocolate bits on top.

Bake for 15 minutes. Reduce the heat to 350°F and bake for another 15 minutes. When done, a toothpick inserted in the center of a brownie should have a few crumbs clinging to it — these brownies should be chewy. Sift powdered sugar over the top while they are still warm.

Let cool slightly. Cut into squares. Store covered.

MAKES ABOUT 16 BROWNIES

☀ *Roll ham, turkey, or roast beef around vegetables such as asparagus, green beans, sliced pepper, celery, carrots, or any other vegetable you might like. You can spread first with cream cheese or mayonnaise.*

ROADSIDE PICNIC #5

* CHICKEN WINGS
* MEAT LOAF SANDWICHES
* ADELE'S POTATO SALAD
* BROCCOLI SALAD
** CHOCOLATE BARS

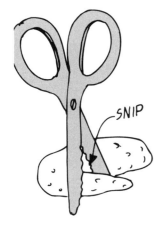
SNIP

CHICKEN WINGS

24 chicken wings (4½ pounds)
1½ teaspoons salt
Freshly ground black pepper
Zest of 1 large orange
3 medium shallots, peeled
1½ cups red currant jelly
2 tablespoons red wine vinegar
1 tablespoon mustard

Fifteen minutes before broiling, set rack 5 inches from heat source and preheat broiler. Have broiler pan ready.

Snip off wing tips with kitchen shears. Place 12 wings, round side down, on broiler pan. Season wings with salt and pepper. Broil until skin begins to brown lightly, about 5 minutes. Use tongs to turn wings over. Season with salt and pepper and broil 5 minutes longer, or until skin begins to brown lightly. Transfer to large bowl. Repeat with remaining wings and seasoning. While wings are broiling, prepare sauce.

Using metal blade in food processor, put orange zest into bowl and turn on machine. Drop shallots through feed tube and process until minced. Add remaining ingredients and process for 5 seconds. Pour sauce over hot wings, cover, and refrigerate overnight, stirring several times.

Place rack in center of oven and preheat to 450°F. Line 2 pans with aluminum foil.

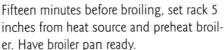

Divide wings and sauce between pans, placing wings round side down. Bake until well browned (about 40 minutes). Turn wings over, brush with sauce in pan, and bake 8 minutes more.

Store in a plastic container and keep in the cooler.

ADELE'S POTATO SALAD

2 pounds boiling potatoes, well cleaned (unpeeled)
¾ cup mayonnaise or plain yogurt
½ cup Dijon mustard
2 garlic cloves, pressed
¼ cup fresh lemon juice
¼ cup olive oil
Salt and freshly ground black pepper to taste
2 bunches scallions
½ cup chopped parsley
1 cucumber, thinly sliced

Boil potatoes. Cool and cut into chunks. Mix mayonnaise, mustard, garlic, lemon juice, olive oil, and salt and pepper in a small bowl. In a larger bowl, mix potatoes, scallions, parsley, and cucumber, and toss with dressing.

Store in a covered plastic container. Keep in cooler until ready to serve.

MAKES 6 TO 8 SERVINGS OR MORE IF A SIDE DISH

ROAD

MEAT LOAF SANDWICHES

1 pound lean ground beef
1 egg
½ cup fine dry bread crumbs
½ onion, chopped
½ cup ready-made spaghetti sauce
Dash of Worcestershire sauce
¼ teaspoon liquid hickory smoke or a dash of hickory powder
Pinch of dried marjoram
Pinch of dried thyme
1 tablespoon chopped fresh parsley
6 slices sourdough bread
Avocado slices (optional)
Tomato slices (optional)

Preheat oven to 350°F. Grease either 2 mini-loaf pans or 1 small loaf pan (about 7½ by 3½ inches).

Place all ingredients except bread, avocado, and tomato in a large bowl. Mix well.

Shape the meat mixture into a loaf and put in pan. Bake for 40 minutes. (If mini-loaf pans are used, check for doneness after 30 minutes; take care that the loaves don't dry out.) Let cool to room temperature. Cover and refrigerate.

Cut 6 slices of the meat loaf. Place meat loaf on a slice of sourdough bread and cover with another slice. Wrap sandwiches and keep in cooler. Store avocado and tomato in a plastic container in cooler. Add a slice of avocado and tomato to your sandwiches at the picnic.

BROCCOLI SALAD

1 large bunch fresh broccoli, blanched
Italian salad dressing (any commercial or homemade variety will do)
2 large tomatoes
1 large onion
1 cup shredded mozzarella cheese

Cut blanched broccoli into bite-sized pieces, place in bowl, and add dressing. Cut up tomatoes and onion, place in another bowl, and add dressing. Marinate both mixtures separately overnight. In the morning, drain the broccoli and the tomatoes and onion, and mix together. Add cheese and refrigerate 3 to 4 hours before serving.

Store in your cooler.

MAKES 4 SERVINGS

CHOCOLATE BARS

1 cup butter or margarine
½ cup packed brown sugar
½ cup granulated sugar
3 egg yolks, beaten
1 tablespoon vanilla extract
2 cups all-purpose unbleached flour
¼ teaspoon salt
¼ teaspoon baking soda
1 cup chocolate chips

Preheat oven to 350°F.

Cream butter and add sugars. Add beaten egg yolks. Mix well. Add remaining ingredients. Bake in a 9- by 11-inch pan for 30 minutes.

Store in individual plastic bags.

MAKES 12 3- BY 2½-INCH BARS

Maggie Moss Tucker travels abroad with her family at least once a year. Maggie highly recommends eating in department stores when traveling with the kids. "What we like about these menus is the wide selection of food 'stations' so the whole family can select choices. Often these European restaurants are on the top floor of the store and offer great views of the city."

133

Pack your cooler with sandwich makings for roadside picnics. No need to assemble the sandwiches ahead of time. They'll go together in a hurry at your picnic site. All you need to do is put out the ingredients and let everyone go to it!

MORE SANDWICHES TO GO

COTTAGE CHEESE AND CARROT PITA

1 cup cottage cheese
⅓ cup grated raw carrots
1 teaspoon sweet pickles, finely chopped
Salt and pepper
1 pita pocket

Mix together the cottage cheese, carrots, and sweet pickles. Season to taste with salt and pepper. Store filling in a plastic container in your cooler. Make sandwiches at your picnic by filling pitas with mixture.

MAKES 1 SANDWICH

CUCUMBER FILLED WITH SALMON SALAD

1 can (15½ ounces) pink salmon, drained
1 package (4 ounces) whipped cream cheese or 1 small package (3 ounces) regular cream cheese
2 tablespoons chopped chives
1 tablespoon fresh chopped parsley
2 tablespoons fresh lemon juice
¼ cup chopped walnuts
1 cucumber, peeled and hollowed out

Mix together all of the ingredients except the cucumber. Stuff cucumber with the salad. Cut into rings and store in a plastic container.

Store in your cooler until ready to serve.

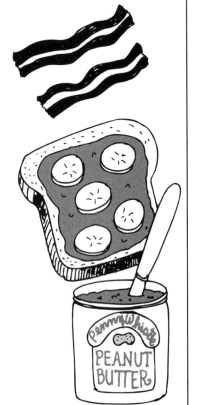

PEANUT BUTTER, BANANA, AND BACON SANDWICH

2 tablespoons peanut butter
2 slices whole-wheat bread
1 lettuce leaf
2 slices bacon, cooked and drained
½ banana, sliced
1 tablespoon cranberry sauce

Spread peanut butter on one slice of bread. Top with lettuce leaf, bacon, and banana. Spread cranberry sauce on other slice of bread and close sandwich.

MAKES 1 SANDWICH

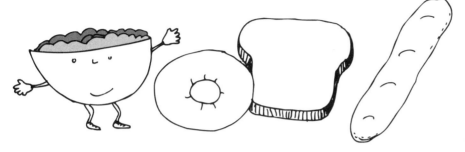

AVOCADO SANDWICH

I small avocado, sliced

I teaspoon fresh lemon juice

2 slices pumpernickel bread

2 slices bacon, cooked and drained

¼ cup spinach leaves,
   well washed and dried

I slice Swiss cheese

⅛ cup alfalfa sprouts

Sprinkle the avocado slices with lemon juice to prevent discoloring. On one slice of bread arrange avocado slices, bacon, spinach leaves, Swiss cheese, and alfalfa sprouts. Close sandwich with other slice of bread.

MAKES I SANDWICH

CHICKEN SANDWICH

I tablespoon apricot jelly

2 slices raisin bread

I lettuce leaf

2 slices roast chicken

Spread jelly on one slice of bread. Top with lettuce leaf and chicken slices. Cover with other slice of bread.

MAKES I SANDWICH

CHICKEN SALAD SANDWICH

¼ cup finely shredded chicken meat

3 tablespoons minced carrots

I tablespoon golden raisins

3 tablespoons plain yogurt

2 slices of your favorite bread

I lettuce leaf

Mix together chicken, carrots, raisins, and yogurt. Spread mixture on one slice of bread. Top with lettuce leaf. Cover with the other slice of bread.

MAKES I SANDWICH

CHEESY SANDWICH

I teaspoon mustard

2 slices rye bread

2 slices Swiss cheese

2 red onion rings

I tomato slice

Spread mustard on one slice of bread. Top with Swiss cheese slices, onion, and tomato. Top with other slice of bread.

MAKES I SANDWICH

Carrot-Raisin Squares are great to pull out of the cooler for munching after your children have had a much needed run around a park after a day's driving. Prepare these squares for your day trip or the first day of a longer journey and store in a cooler.

I cup grated carrots

3 tablespoons mayonnaise

½ cup chopped unsalted nuts
   (peanuts or walnuts are best)

I tablespoon fresh lemon juice

¼ teaspoon salt

Drop of Worcestershire sauce

2 to 4 slices cinnamon-raisin bread

In a bowl, mix all of the ingredients except the bread. Cover and chill for as long as you can (but even 5 or 10 minutes will do).

Spread the carrot mixture on the bread. Cover. Cut each sandwich into 4 squares and wrap well.

LIQUID AND DRY MEASURE EQUIVALENCIES

Customary	Metric
¼ teaspoon	1.25 milliliters
½ teaspoon	2.5 milliliters
1 teaspoon	5 milliliters
1 tablespoon	15 milliliters
1 fluid ounce	30 milliliters
¼ cup	60 milliliters
⅓ cup	80 milliliters
½ cup	120 milliliters
1 cup	240 milliliters
1 pint (2 cups)	480 milliliters
1 quart (4 cups)	960 milliliters (.96 liters)
1 gallon (4 quarts)	3.84 liters
1 ounce (by weight)	28 grams
¼ pound (4 ounces)	114 grams
1 pound (16 ounces)	454 grams
2.2 pounds	1 kilogram (100 grams)

OVEN TEMPERATURE EQUIVALENCIES

Description	°Fahrenheit	°Celsius
Cool	200	90
Very slow	250	120
Slow	300-325	150-160
Moderately slow	325-350	160-180
Moderate	350-375	180-190
Moderately hot	375-400	190-200
Hot	400-450	200-230
Very Hot	450-500	230-260

Resources

Museums for Children to Visit

SPORTS MUSEUMS

THE BASKETBALL HALL OF FAME, Springfield, Massachusetts

THE NATIONAL FOOTBALL HALL OF FAME, New Brunswick, New Jersey

THE NATIONAL BASEBALL HALL OF FAME, Cooperstown, New York

THE NATIONAL PROFESSIONAL FOOTBALL HALL OF FAME, Canton, Ohio

PETER J. McGOVERN LITTLE LEAGUE MUSEUM, Williamsport, Pennsylvania

THE HOCKEY HALL OF FAME, Toronto, Ontario

★ ALL THE MUSEUMS ARE LISTED IN ALPHABETICAL ORDER ACCORDING TO STATE.

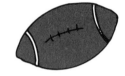

DOLL MUSEUMS

ANGEL'S ATTIC, Santa Monica, California

DENVER MUSEUM OF MINIATURES, DOLLS AND TOYS, Denver, Colorado

TOY AND MINIATURE MUSEUM, Kansas City, Missouri

STRONG MUSEUM, Rochester, New York
   (This is not a doll museum but it contains a permanent collection of dolls and toys.)

WASHINGTON DOLLS' HOUSE AND TOY MUSEUM, Washington, D.C.

AIR & SPACE MUSEUMS

U.S. SPACE AND ROCKET CENTER, Huntsville, Alabama

PIMA AIR AND SPACE MUSEUM, Tucson, Arizona

NAVAL AVIATION MUSEUM, Pensacola, Florida

AIR FORCE MUSEUM, Wright-Patterson Air Force Base, Columbus, Ohio

EAA MUSEUM, Whitman Field, Oshkosh, Wisconsin

SMITHSONIAN AIR & SPACE MUSEUM, Washington, D.C.

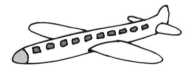

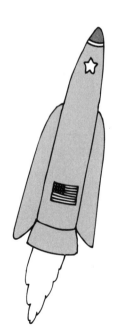

NATURAL HISTORY MUSEUMS

LOS ANGELES COUNTY MUSEUM OF NATURAL HISTORY, Los Angeles, California

THE GEORGE C. PAGE MUSEUM OF LA BREA DISCOVERIES, Los Angeles, California

SAN DIEGO NATURAL HISTORY MUSEUM, Balboa Park, San Diego, California

DENVER MUSEUM OF NATURAL HISTORY, Denver, Colorado

PEABODY MUSEUM OF NATURAL HISTORY, Yale University, New Haven, Connecticut

DINOSAUR STATE PARK, Rocky Hill, Connecticut

MUSEUM OF NATURAL HISTORY, Marathon, Florida

FIELD MUSEUM OF NATURAL HISTORY, Chicago, Illinois

SCIENCE MUSEUM OF MINNESOTA, St. Paul, Minnesota

MUSEUM OF THE ROCKIES, Montana State University, Bozeman, Montana

AMERICAN MUSEUM OF NATURAL HISTORY, New York, New York

NATURAL HISTORY MUSEUM, Cleveland, Ohio

CARNEGIE MUSEUM OF NATURAL HISTORY, Pittsburgh, Pennsylvania

DINOSAUR NATIONAL MONUMENT, Jensen, Utah

UTAH MUSEUM OF NATURAL HISTORY, University of Utah, Salt Lake City, Utah

MILWAUKEE PUBLIC MUSEUM, Milwaukee, Wisconsin

FOSSIL BUTTE NATIONAL MONUMENT, Kemmerer, Wyoming

EXPLORERS' HALL, Headquarters of National Geographic Society, Washington, D.C.

NATIONAL MUSEUM OF NATURAL HISTORY, Smithsonian Institution, Washington, D.C.

TYRELL MUSEUM OF PALEONTOLOGY, Drumheller, Alberta, Canada

Terry Bilsky suggests that if you are traveling near the water, try to eat in waterside places. Kids love watching the boats and seagulls, and sometimes you may find a balcony they can play on when sitting at the table becomes a chore.

CHILDREN'S MUSEUMS

CHILDREN'S HANDS-ON MUSEUM, Tuscaloosa, Alabama

TUCSON CHILDREN'S MUSEUM, Tucson, Arizona

LOS ANGELES CHILDREN'S MUSEUM, Los Angeles, California

KIDSPACE MUSEUM, Pasadena, California

VISIONARIUM CHILDREN'S MUSEUM, Sacramento, California

THE CHILDREN'S MUSEUM OF SAN DIEGO, San Diego, California

CHILDREN'S DISCOVERY MUSEUM OF SAN JOSE, San Jose, California

THE CHILDREN'S MUSEUM OF DENVER, Denver, Colorado

EXPLORATIONS V, Lakeland, Florida

MIAMI YOUTH MUSEUM, Miami, Florida

JUNIOR MUSEUM OF BAY COUNTY, Panama City, Florida

CHILDREN'S MUSEUM OF TAMPA, Tampa, Florida

EXPLORATION STATION CHILDREN'S MUSEUM, Bradley, Illinois

CHICAGO CHILDREN'S MUSEUM, Chicago, Illinois

CHILDREN'S MUSEUM OF ILLINOIS, Decatur, Illinois

QUAD CITY KIDS & COMPANY, Moline, Illinois

DISCOVERY CENTER MUSEUM, Rockford, Illinois

DUPAGE CHILDREN'S MUSEUM, Wheaton, Illinois

KOHL CHILDREN'S MUSEUM, Wilmette, Illinois

THE CHILDREN'S MUSEUM, Indianapolis, Indiana

HANNAH LINDAHL CHILDREN'S MUSEUM, Mishawaka, Indiana

THE CHILDREN'S MUSEUM, Bettendorf, Iowa

CHILDREN'S MUSEUM, Kansas City, Kansas

LOUISIANA CHILDREN'S MUSEUM, New Orleans, Louisiana

CHILDREN'S MUSEUM OF MAINE, Portland, Maine

THE BALTIMORE CHILDREN'S MUSEUM AT THE CLOISTERS, Brooklandville, Maryland

THE CHILDREN'S DISCOVERY MUSEUM, Acton, Massachusetts

CHILDREN'S MUSEUM, Boston, Massachusetts

CHILDREN'S MUSEUM AT HOLYOKE, Holyoke, Massachusetts

ANN ARBOR HANDS-ON MUSEUM, Ann Arbor, Michigan

CHILDREN'S MUSEUM, Flint, Michigan

MINNESOTA CHILDREN'S MUSEUM, St. Paul, Minnesota

MAGIC HOUSE, St. Louis, Missouri

LINCOLN CHILDREN'S MUSEUM, Lincoln, Nebraska

OMAHA CHILDREN'S MUSEUM, Omaha, Nebraska

LIED DISCOVERY CHILDREN'S MUSEUM, Las Vegas, Nevada

MONADNOCK CHILDREN'S MUSEUM, Keene, New Hampshire

CHILDREN'S MUSEUM OF PORTSMOUTH, Portsmouth, New Hampshire

NEW JERSEY CHILDREN'S MUSEUM, Paramus, New Jersey

SANTA FE CHILDREN'S MUSEUM, Santa Fe, New Mexico

BROOKLYN CHILDREN'S MUSEUM, Brooklyn, New York

CHILDREN'S MUSEUM OF MANHATTAN, New York, New York

THE CHILDREN'S MUSEUM AT SARATOGA, Saratoga Springs, New York

STATEN ISLAND CHILDREN'S MUSEUM, Staten Island, New York

UTICA CHILDREN'S MUSEUM, Utica, New York

DISCOVERY PLACE, Charlotte, North Carolina

THE CHILDREN'S MUSEUM AT YUNKER FARM, Fargo, North Dakota

CLEVELAND CHILDREN'S MUSEUM, Cleveland, Ohio

SOUTHERN OREGON HISTORICAL SOCIETY CHILDREN'S MUSEUM,
    Jacksonville, Oregon

PORTLAND CHILDREN'S MUSEUM, Portland, Oregon

GILBERT HOUSE CHILDREN'S MUSEUM, Salem, Oregon

PLEASE TOUCH MUSEUM, Philadelphia, Pennsylvania

PITTSBURGH CHILDREN'S MUSEUM, Pittsburgh, Pennsylvania

CHILDREN'S MUSEUM OF RHODE ISLAND, Pawtucket, Rhode Island

CHILDREN'S MUSEUM OF MEMPHIS, Memphis, Tennessee

CHILDREN'S MUSEUM OF OAK RIDGE, Oak Ridge, Tennessee

AUSTIN CHILDREN'S MUSEUM, Austin, Texas

CHILDREN'S MUSEUM OF HOUSTON, Houston, Texas

LAREDO CHILDREN'S MUSEUM, Laredo, Texas

CHILDREN'S MUSEUM IN NEW BRAUNFELS, New Braunfels, Texas

CHILDREN'S MUSEUM OF UTAH, Salt Lake City, Utah

VIRGINIA DISCOVERY MUSEUM, Charlottesville, Virginia

RICHMOND CHILDREN'S MUSEUM, Richmond, Virginia

SEATTLE CHILDREN'S MUSEUM, Seattle, Washington

MADISON'S CHILDREN'S MUSEUM, Madison, Wisconsin

CAPITAL CHILDREN'S MUSEUM OF NATIONAL LEARNING CENTER,
    Washington, D.C.

★ You may be surprised, but many children like museums, as long as you involve them in choosing the subjects. Fourteen-year-old veteran traveler Julia Boorstin's advice: Make the visits short!

★ When the Boorstins went to the Louvre in Paris (Julia was 14 and Adam 9), they thought it was going to be a battle, but it turned out to be the best museum visit ever. Remembers Paul, "Julia had just finished a European history course and was enthralled by seeing all the art of the Greeks and the Renaissance that she had studied in books. Adam was interested in the many crucifixion paintings. He became fascinated with the different ways artists depicted the blood and the pain. Expert Adam was able to tell us which depictions were realistic and which were not."

SCIENCE MUSEUMS

THE EXPLOREUM MUSEUM, Mobile, Alabama

PALO ALTO JUNIOR MUSEUM & ZOO, Palo Alto, California

THE REUBEN H. FLEET SPACE THEATER & SCIENCE CENTER, San Diego, California

EXPLORATORIUM, San Francisco, California

THE DISCOVERY MUSEUM, Bridgeport, Connecticut

GREAT EXPLORATIONS, St. Petersburg, Florida

THE DISCOVERY CENTER OF IDAHO, Boise, Idaho

SCIENCE STATION, Cedar Rapids, Iowa

OMNISPHERE & SCIENCE CENTER, Wichita, Kansas

IMPRESSION 5 SCIENCE MUSEUM, Lansing, Michigan

LIBERTY SCIENCE CENTER, Jersey City, New Jersey

NEW YORK HALL OF SCIENCE, Corona, New York

SONY WONDER TECHNOLOGY LAB, New York, New York

CUMBERLAND SCIENCE MUSUEM, Nashville, Tennessee

DISCOVERY PLACE, Charlotte, North Carolina

THE FRANKLIN INSTITUTE, Philadelphia, Pennsylvania

SOUTH DAKOTA DISCOVERY CENTER & AQUARIUM, Pierre, South Dakota

DON HARRINGTON DISCOVERY CENTER, Amarillo, Texas

DISCOVERY MUSEUM, Essex Junction, Vermont

MONTSHIRE MUSEUM, Norwich, Vermont

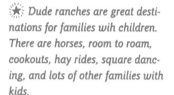

⭐ Dude ranches are great destinations for families wih children. There are horses, room to roam, cookouts, hay rides, square dancing, and lots of other families with kids.

Travel Resources

If your kids want to go to a dude ranch, write to Dude Ranchers Association, Box 471, La Porte, CO 80535, for information.

Call Go Camping America's toll-free hotline (800) 47-SUNNY for a free "Camping Vacation Planner" — a resource guide of useful advice and RV information.

Oregon Trail Coordinating Council, can be reached by phoning (503) 22-TRAIL

Some camps operate family programs. Call (800) 428-2267 to order the American Camping Association's *Guide to Accredited Camps* for $12.95.

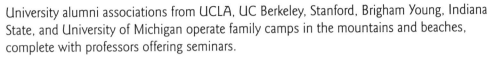

University alumni associations from UCLA, UC Berkeley, Stanford, Brigham Young, Indiana State, and University of Michigan operate family camps in the mountains and beaches, complete with professors offering seminars.

The 1993 KOA directory listing all their campgrounds is available by sending $3 to Kampgrounds of America, Inc., Executive Offices, Dept. FA, P.O. Box 30558, Billings, MT 59114-0558.

For the *Campground & RV Service Directory,* send $12.95 to Trailer Life, Dept. FA, 29901 Agoura Rd., Agoura, CA 91301, or call (818) 991-4980.

Write to the natural resources or travel bureaus of the states you would like to visit for information and directories of campsites including state parks.

For information on national parks, write the U.S Dept. of the Interior, National Park Service, P.O. Box 37127, Washington, DC 20013-7127.

TWYCH (Travel with Your Children), 45 W. 18th Street, New York, NY 10011, (212) 206-0688. This advisory service for families traveling with children publishes a newsletter, *Family Travel Times* (10 times a year), *Cruising with Children, Skiing with Children,* and an *Airline Guide.*

The National Association of Cruise Only Agencies, at P.O. Box 7209, Freeport, NY 11520, provides listings of regional cruise agencies.

The National Geographic Catalog is available by calling (800) 447-0647.

Overseas Adventure Travel of Cambridge, Massachusetts, explores exotic trips for family adventures; call (800) 221-0814.

Wilderland Adventures in Seattle, Washington, also provides itineraries for exotic trips; call (800) 345-HIKE.

American Wilderness Experience, Boulder, Colorado, an adventure travel company; call (800) 444-0099.

For the pamphlet "Recreational Opportunities on Public Lands: An Invitation to Enjoyment," write to Office of the Outdoor Recreation Initiative, U.S. Dept. of the Interior, Washington, DC 20240.

For house exchanges, contact either of the following: Vacation Exchange Club, P.O. Box 650, Key West, FL 33041; (800) 638-3841, or Intervac U.S. International Home Exchange, P.O. Box 590504, San Francisco, CA 94159, (800) 756-HOME. You pay a modest fee and your home is listed with others around the world. You make the match. Agencies do not check out homes.

For VIP passes to the White House, Capitol, FBI Building, Kennedy Center, and U.S. Senate or House buildings, write your Senator at U.S. Senate, Washington, DC 20510, or your Congressman at U.S. House of Representatives, Washington, DC 20515. For more information about White House tours, contact the White House Visitor's Office at (202) 456-2322.

Take the kids to places that take them back in time to history they have studied. Julia Boorstin was 11 when she visited Williamsburg, Virginia, and loved getting dressed up in colonial clothes and playing with colonial dolls. Her brother, Adam, who was 6, was captivated by the conversations he had with the actors playing a ship's captain and a slave. While wandering around, he discovered a Revolutionary War soldiers' encampment. Adam was ready to stay there forever!

143

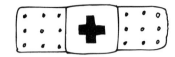

Health Resources

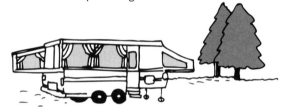

Call American Academy of Pediatrics at (800) 433-9016 for a doctor in the areas in which you will be traveling.

The Skin Cancer Foundation provides a list of sunscreens that have its Seal of Recommendation. Write 245 Fifth Avenue, Suite 2402, New York, NY 10016.

The Pocket Doctor by Stephen Bezruchka, M.D. (The Mountaineers, 1992). Lots of information about traveling in good health. $4.95.

For a copy of *Traveling Healthy*, send a self-addressed, stamped business-size envelope to 10848 70th Road, Forest Hills, NY 11375.

International Association for Medical Assistance to Travelers Directory. This directory of English-speaking doctors is available free by writing IAMAT, 417 Center Street, Lewiston, NY 14092; a nonprofit organization.

Travel Guides for Parents

Adventuring with Children: The Family Pack-Along Guide to the Outdoors and the World by Nan Jeffrey with Kevin Jeffrey (San Francisco: Foghorn Press, 1992).

The Amusement Park Guide by Tim O'Brien (Chester, CT: Globe Pequot Press, 1991).

The Best Bargain Family Vacations in the U.S.A. by Laura Sutherland and Valerie Wolf Deutsch (New York: St. Martin's Press, 1993). Lists 250 affordable vacation spots for families.

Best Places to Go: A Family Destination Guide by Nan Jeffrey (San Francisco: Foghorn Press, 1993).

Doing Children's Museums: A Guide to 265 Hands-on Museums, by Joanne Cleaver (Charlotte, VT: Williamson Publishing, 1992).

Family Sports Adventures: Exciting Vacations for Parents & Kids to Share by Megan Stine (Boston: Sports Illustrated for Kids, 1991).

Family Travel by Evelyn Kaye (Boulder, CO: Blue Penguin Publications, 1993).

The Family Travel Guides Catalogue: Books for the Traveling Family. A catalogue of family travel books, game books, and audio cassettes. Send $1 for postage and handling or a long self-addressed stamped envelope to P.O. Box 6061, Albany, CA 94706-0061, or call (510) 527-5849.

Fielding's Europe with Children by Leila Hadley (New York: William Morrow, 1984).

⭐ *When the Anthony family, from Wellesley, Massachusetts, went to the Louvre in Paris, they had sons Drew and Graham look for the real Ninja Turtle artists — Donatello, Raphael, Michelangelo, and Leonardo. The kids were totally focused as they made their way throughout the museum galleries, searching for their heroes. Now that's turtle power!*

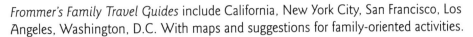

Frommer's Family Travel Guides include California, New York City, San Francisco, Los Angeles, Washington, D.C. With maps and suggestions for family-oriented activities.

Great Resorts for Parents and Kids: A Travel Guide to U.S. Resorts with Supervised Children's Programs by Gayle Barker and Joanna Pinick (Seattle: Editor's Ink, 1990).

Great Vacations with Your Kids by Dorothy Jordan and Marjorie Adoff Cohen (New York: Penguin Books, 1987).

How to Take Great Trips with Your Kids by Sanford and Joan Portnoy (Boston: The Harvard Common Press, 1983).

Innocents Abroad: Traveling with Kids in Europe by Valerie Wolf Deutsch and Laura Sutherland (New York: Penguin, 1991). Covers twelve countries and offers advice on getting there, customs, and what to do.

Kids on Board: A 10-City Guide to Great American Family Vacations by Ken and Marilyn Wilson (New York: Warner Books, 1994).

My RV/Camping Travel Planner and Trip Diary. Available from Career Press, P.O. Box 34, Hawthorne, NJ 07506; or call (800) 227-3371.

North American Aircraft and Aerospace Museum Guide edited by Ronald B. Stone (Tulsa, OK: Bruce/Beeson Publishers, 1992). Available from the publishers, 2428 East 56th Place, Tulsa, OK 74105.

Recommended Family Inns of America, by the authors of the Recommended Country Inn series (Chester, CT: Globe Pequot Press, 1989).

Recommended Family Resorts in the United States, Canada, and the Caribbean: 100 Quality Resorts with Leisure Activities for Children and Adults by Jane Wilford with Janet Tice (Chester, CT: Globe Pequot Press, 1990). Globe Pequot Press also offers a free catalogue of quality travel books. Write to them at Box Q, Chester, CT 06412.

Super Family Vacations Resort and Adventure Guide by Martha Shirk and Nancy Klepper (New York: HarperCollins, 1992). Covers U.S., Canada, and the Caribbean.

Travel with Children by Maureen Wheeler (Berkeley: Lonely Planet Publications, 1985). For other guidebooks, write to Embarcadero West, 112 Linden Street, Oakland CA 94607.

Traveling with Children and Enjoying It by Arlene Kay Butler. (Chester, CT: Globe Pequot Press, 1991).

Trouble-Free Travel with Children: Helpful Hints for Parents on the Go by Vicki Lansky (Deephaven, MN: The Book Peddlers, 1985).

The U.S. Dept. of Education publishes the 26-page booklet *Helping Your Child Learn Geography.* Send a check or money order for 50 cents to Geography, Consumer Information Center, Pueblo, CO 81009.

U.S. News's 1993 Great Vacation Drives. Send check or money order for $8.95 to U.S. News, c/o Sisk Fulfillment Services, P.O. Box 470, Federalsburg, MD 21632; or call (800) 445-7500 for credit card orders.

What to Do with the Kids This Year: One Hundred Family Vacation Places with Time Off for You! by Jane Wilford and Janet Tice (Charlotte, NC: The East Woods Press, 1986).

★ *Ellen Meyer took daughters Jennifer and Sarah, then 12 and 15, up to their friends' ranch in Montana. Rather than taking them riding, Ellen decided to introduce them to something new and unexpected — fly fishing. At first, the girls grimaced, figuring that this was not a sport for them. But with a little prodding, they found themselves standing in the river in waders, each holding a fishing pole in her hands, happy as can be. The motto? Says Ellen, "Never underestimate the power of introducing your children to the most unlikely activities."*

Children's Travel Resources

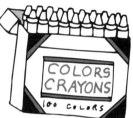

ACTIVITY BOOKS & ACCESSORIES

AAA Travel Activity Book: The Official AAA Fun Book for Kids by Tom Koken, Jane Lipp, and Kathleen Paton (New York: Checkerboard Press, 1991).

ALEX manufactures prepackaged craft kits that are great for traveling. Write P.O. Box 391, New York, NY 10038.

"Are We There Yet?": Travel Games for Kids by Richard Salter (New York: Crown, 1991).

Around the World: Activity Play Book with Stickers (Dominguez Hills, CA: Educational Insights, 1988). Also from Educational Insights, *Around the U.S.A.: Activity Play Book with Stickers* by Sally Palow (1991).

Beach by Susan Baum and Harriet Ziefert (New York: HarperCollins, 1991). Picture book with reusable stickers to place on illustrations, or make your own. Also look for *City Shapes*.

The Book of Classic Games (Palo Alto, CA: Klutz Press). Book of playing boards for fifteen games. Includes dice and game pieces. Call (415) 424-0739.

Create Your Own Beach Sticker Picture by Robbie Stillerman (Toronto: Dover, 1993).

Dot to Dot at the Seaside by Karen Bryant-Mole (London: Usborne Publishing, Ltd., 1993).

Flags of the United Nations Sticker Book by Jan and Frank Asch and Sue Leland (New York: Scholastic, 1990).

Games for Travel by Richard Latta (Los Angeles: Price Stern Sloan, 1976). Games and puzzles.

Illustory. Your child can write and illustrate pages that are then typeset and bound into a beautiful book. $19.95. Chimeric Inc., P.O. Box 101149, Denver, CO 80250; or call (303) 321-0721.

Kids Travel: A Backseat Survival Kit by the editors of Klutz Press (Palo Alto, CA: Klutz Press, 1994).

Kid's Trip Diary. An 80-page softcover book includes tips on vacation preparation, trip diary, puzzles and games, a section for memories of your trip, and a diary divided into categories — what I did today, etc. Call Magellan's, (800) 962-4943.

Kid's Vacation Diary (St. Paul, MN: Marlor Press, Inc., 1991). Includes sections on getting ready for your trip, what to do on the road, games, and memories of trip.

Mad Dash! Three Minutes Across America. Players have 3 minutes to make trails of states across the U.S.A. For ages 8 and up. Write ITOS Enterprises, R.D. 3, Box 300, York, PA 17402.

Make a Family Video Album. Videotape that instructs your family on making the perfect video album. $19.95. Produced by Christopher Stanton for Edgewater Productions,

Map Coloring Book: Countries and Flags (Cambridge, MA: InterArts, Ltd., 1992). Sections on learning to make maps and chart a course, world flags, and much more. Call (617) 354-4655.

Miles of Smiles: 101 Great Car Games & Activities by Carole Terwilliger Meyers (Albany, CA: Carousel Press, 1992).

My Crazy and Wacky Travel Adventures: A Kid's Travel Journal and Playbook by Kelsey B. Lynn, age 10 (Rensselaer, NY: Hamilton, 1991). Includes games, maps, and a diary for recording each day's events.

My First Camera Book by Anne Kostick (New York: Workman, 1989). Introductory book to photography with instructions on cameras and photo ideas; includes photo album. Comes with reusable fixed-focus camera (uses 110 film).

My World and Globe, by Ira Wolfman (New York: Workman, 1992). A kit including an inflatable globe, stickers to put on the globe, and book explaining everything from map making to time changes. $12.95.

Press & Peel U.S.A. Map (Denmark: Uniset, 1985).
Vinyl figures and map pieces can be used over and over.

Rand McNally: *Rand McNally Children's World Atlas* ($14.95); and *Randy McNally Backseat Books: On Vacation!* ($1.95); *Kids' U.S. Road Atlas* ($3.95); *Are We There Yet?* ($3.95); *Best Activity Book Ever;* also Randy McNally Kids' Maps for Florida, Texas, California, United States. Order from Rand McNally & Co., P.O. Box 7606, Chicago, IL 60680; or call (800) 234-0679.

Read a Mat — Eat and Learn. A series of vinyl placemats includes the United States, the world, and the solar system. $3.50.

Sealed with a Kiss. Travel kits full of games, puzzles, and crafts for children 3½ and older. $30. Call (800) 888-SWAK or (301) 468-2604.

Stick & Lift U.S.A. Map and *Stick & Lift World Map*. Reusable vinyl figures can be moved around on maps. Order from Safari, Ltd., Miami, FL 33163.

Travel Activities: Fun for Kids on the Move (New York: Checkerboard Press, 1990).

Travel Games for Kids by Andrew Langley (Stockbridge, MA: Berkshire House, 1993).

USA Bingo. Different variations on the standard bingo game include capital bingo, state nickname bingo, trivia, and postal abbreviation bingo.
Write Trend Enterprises, St. Paul, MN 55164.

Some transcontinental flights have individual video screens and recorders at each seat. When Bryn Lander Simon went to Ireland with her parents, she was able to choose from a library of children's videos. Two movies later (and a little nap along the way), the plane landed with Bryn as happy as can be.

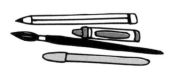

The Usborne Book of Air Travel Games by Moira Butterfield (London: Usborne Publishing, Ltd., 1986).

The Usborne Book of Car Travel Games by Tony Potter (London: Usborne Publishing, Ltd., 1986).

Usborne Superpuzzles: Map & Maze Puzzles by Sarah Dixon and Radhi Parekh (London: Usborne Publishing, Ltd., 1993).

The World's Best Travel Games by Sheila Anne Barry (New York: Sterling Publishing Co., Inc., 1987).

The World's Greatest Travel Game. Play seven different games and try to make up your own with this cube game. Woodkrafter Kits, Yarmouth, MN.

Zippered U.S. map from Rand McNally, (800) 234-0679, is a cotton bag that unzips to become a map of the United States with multicolored, soft-sculpture states that fasten with Velcro to proper locations.

"FIRST FLIGHT" STORY BOOKS

This is a list of books about a child's trip on an airplane for the first time — either alone or with his family.

First Flight by David McPhail (Boston: Little, Brown, 1987). A little boy flies by himself to visit his grandmother.

Going on a Plane by Anne Civardi and Stephen Cartwright (London: Usborne Publishing, Ltd., 1988). Follow the Tripp family as they prepare for their vacation, go to the airport, fly on the plane, and arrive at their destination.

Kitty's First Airplane Trip by Linda C. Falken (New York: Scholastic, 1993). A young boy flies with his cat and his mother to New York.

We're Taking an Airplane Trip by Dinah L. Moché (New York: Western Publishing, 1982). Elizabeth and Jimmy Baldwin fly to visit their grandparents without their parents.

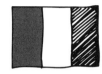

TRAVEL GUIDES JUST FOR KIDS

A Kid's Guide to Washington, D.C., by Diane C. Clark; *A Kid's Guide to Florida* by Karen Grove; *A Kid's Guide to Southern California.* All published by Harcourt Brace Jovanovich, Inc., New York, NY, as part of Gulliver Travels travel guide series written for children, with facts, maps, games, diaries, puzzles, and more.

First Book of France by Louisa Somerville (London: Usborne Publishing, Ltd., 1989). A child's guide including maps, sightseeing, and activity suggestions.

Getting to Know France and French by Nicola Wright; *Getting to Know Spain and Spanish* by Janet De Saules; *Getting to Know Germany and German* by Janine Amos; *Getting to Know Italy and Italian* by Emma Sansone. All published by Barron's Educational Series, Inc., Hauppauge, NY. 1993.

Insight Guides. Guides for teen-agers covering a city or country's history and culture. Paperback volumes about $19.95.

Kidding Around series, with books covering San Francisco, San Diego, Seattle, Atlanta, Philadelphia, Washington, D.C., Santa Fe, the Hawaiian Islands, New York City, Chicago, and Boston. John Muir Publications, P.O. Box 613, Santa Fe, NM 87504; (800) 888-7504.

Let's Go Traveling by Robin Rector Krupp. (New York: Morrow Jr. Books, 1992). Rachel Rose goes off to six ancient sites. Illustrations are collages of her diary, postcards, pictures, and more.

Let's Visit Britain: A Passport Sticker Book by David Gantz (New York: Simon & Schuster, 1989). Follow Frannie and Joey as they tour Britain. Comes with stickers and a souvenir "Passport Book."

The Usborne Book of London: History, Buildings, People. Things to Do and See by Moira Butterfield (London: Usborne Publishing, Ltd., 1987).

ROAD TAPES

Cars, Boats, Trains, Planes, and Other Things That Go from Kidsongs Kids, Warner Brothers. Tunes about "things that go" sung by a chorus of children. $8.

Car Songs: Songs to Sing Anywhere by Dennis Buck. Also *On the Road Again: More Car Songs*. Kimbo, Box 477, Long Branch, NJ 07740.

Comprehensive Communications, Inc. Auto Tape Tours, P.O. Box 227/2 Elbrook Drive, Allendale, NJ 07401; (201) 236-1666. Catalogue of travel-related audio and video tapes. Also lists books on tape for adults and children.

Games for the Road (40-minute cassette tape), *Games for the Road Book* (15-page illustrated book), *More Games for the Road* (40-minute cassette tape), *More Games Activity Book* (20-page illustrated book), all by D. Valentine. These tapes feature educational, entertaining, noncompetitive games for kids ages 5 and up. $9.95, plus $1.50 postage and handling. Valentine Productions, 3856 Grand Forest Dr., Norcross, GA 30092; (800) 544-8322 (call for free catalogue).

Imagination Cruise by Chris Holder, A Gentle Wind. Story and songs, ages 5-11. $7.95.

The Kids' Car Songbook and Audiocassette. $9.95 plus $2.50 postage and handling. Running Press, 125 South 22nd Street, Philadelphia, PA 19103; (800) 345-5359.

Ride with Me and *Hopping Around from Place to Place*, tapes with tunes for all types of travel, ages 4 to 7. $10.99. Ella Jenkins Educational Activities, Inc.; (800) 677-7760.

Sing Along as You Ride Along (book and tape). $5.95 plus $2.23 postage and handling. Practical Parenting, Dept. S.TR, Deephaven, MN, 55391; (800) 255-3379 (call for free catalogue).

Take Me with You! by Peter Alsop, Yellow Moon Press. $9.95. Folk songs, ages 4–8.

Traffic Jams and Songs for the Car by Joe Scruggs, Shadow Play Records, Includes tunes such as "Buckle Up," "Car Seat Exercise," and "Speed Bump Blues." Order from Educational Graphics Press, P.O. Box 180476, Austin, TX 78718.

Travelin' Magic: Contemporary and Traditional Travelin' Tunes by Joanie Bartels, Discovery Music. One side of this tape is devoted to instrumentals, the other has vocals.

Woof Hits the Road! by Bill Wellington, Alcazar Records. Radio station WOOF is a silly way to pass the time. $10.

We have included the following pages to help
you and your family start your own travel journal.
Just photocopy and you're ready to go.

BON VOYAGE!

Emergency Numbers

NAME   PHONE NUMBER

Packing List

1. _____
2. _____
3. _____
4. _____
5. _____
6. _____
7. _____
8. _____
9. _____
10. _____
11. _____
12. _____
13. _____
14. _____
15. _____
16. _____
17. _____
18. _____
19. _____
20. _____

Favorite New Places

_____

_____

_____

_____

_____

_____

Favorite New Foods

_____

_____

_____

_____

_____

_____

 New Friends

NAME   ADDRESS   PHONE

Diary Notes

Diary Notes

Diary Notes

★ *Certificate of Excellence* ★

_____

RECEIVES THIS AWARD FOR EXCELLENCE IN

_____

_____

_____

_____

_____   _____
SIGNATURE   DATE

_____
WITNESS